THE ART OF PROFESSIONAL SALES

HANDBOOK FOR THE CAREER SELLER

CRAIG RAINEY

Craig Rainey Publishing
AUSTIN, TEXAS

Craig Rainey / Craig Rainey Publishing
Austin, Texas
craig@craigrainey.com
www.craigrainey.com

Ordering Information:
Quantity sales. Special discounts are available on quantity purchases by corporations, associations, and others. For details, contact us at the email address: craig@craigrainey.com

The Art of Professional Sales / Craig Rainey. —1st ed.
ISBN 978-1-7339867-9-3

For My Dearest Alexandra, My Inspiration, and my Muse

High pressure and pushy tactics are the stock and trade of the aggressive amateur.

—CRAIG RAINEY

Contents

FOREWORD

I DECIDED TO WRITE A SALES TRAINING BOOK because I saw that the art of sales was disappearing from most business models. I am not referring to the pursuit of sales numbers. Every business owner and entrepreneur gives lip service to the importance of sales. To each of these leaders in industry, sales has become a statistical event only. Businesses nowadays seem to relegate their sales numbers to the same circumstance of chance they assign outside production activities to the weather.

I see the art of professional selling abandoned by so many. Most sellers, and buyers, consider traditional sales an antiquated practice which no longer works. In the modern age of an informed customer base, and the emergence of compassionate business ownership, sales is considered a discourtesy.

TODAY COMPANY OWNERS FOCUS EVERY ASPECT OF THEIR BUSINESS ON SOCIAL MEDIA POPULARITY AND 5-STAR REVIEWS. THE POSSIBILITY THAT THEIR SALES DEPARTMENT MIGHT BLUNDER INTO PROFESSIONAL SELLING AND POTENTIALLY PRESSURE A CUSTOMER INTO BUYING TERRIFIES THEM.

A part of my preparation for writing this book included searching brick and mortar bookstores and scanning online book retailers for sales training books. I am astounded at how few sales training books are available. I found a few of the standards: Napoleon Hill, Zig

Ziglar, and W. Clement Stone, but there were few recently published books on the true art of selling.

Most of what I found centered around celebrity sales phenoms and how they achieved their unprecedented sales numbers. Other books focused upon the psychology of how to avoid upsetting customers while trying to implement carefully guarded persuasion skills. I saw none that taught professional selling techniques in the context of today's sophisticated market.

If you have read some of the books available today, you may be surprised at the tone the authors take with their readers. It seems to me that many sales manual writers assume the role of the scolding manager or an impatient parent.

I read a recently published sales book, penned by a currently well-known sales trainer. The book was written from the perspective that sales is hard and if the reader would just toughen up a little, he or she could learn how to do it. Just browsing the table of contents, even the chapter titles seemed a bit condescending.

As we seasoned veterans age in the sales profession, we must be wary of the onset of cynicism towards young people today. It is easy to talk down to a group based upon preconceived notions or from a sense of superiority and prestige.

As a matter of course, my generation tends to discount the modern generation. People my age feel, as does every previous generation, that we have endured more hardships, and worked more ardently towards our goals, than "kids nowadays."

I try to keep the painful memories of my early sales fears, and my difficulties in learning the craft, handy when I write for my reader. Like you, there was a time when the sales process was intimidating to me.

I don't believe that deprecation and belittling is an effective means by which to connect with a reader. Many of the sales books I purchased during my preparation read like a genius talking down to a dullard. When I see the words "merely" or "you just have to do this" in a book, or in the style of writing a book, I am immediately turned off. The process may be simple, but it is not easy. If it were, everyone would be able to do it, and there would be no premium paid for those who excel.

In the sales business, the most obvious difference between the hardships of the past and those of today is the cause of the hardship. In the early years of my sales career, the difficulties centered around learning techniques and applying them to the sales presentation. Today, the hardships are those related to finding a sales position where you can actually learn and use professional sales techniques without being criticized by the fearful and the unknowledgeable. Today, the packaging of the sale is the focus, not the ability to make a sale consistently and predictably.

THE SELLER WHO EMPLOYS PROFESSIONAL SALES TOOLS, WILL OUTPERFORM THE SELLER WHO ONLY PRACTICES SALES PROFESSIONALLY.

No matter the social or economic pressures affecting a person, I believe in his or her innate values and strengths. If you purchased this book, you are a cut above. I believe that if you take the time to learn what I offer you in this book, you are to be respected.

Do I consider my reader a member of a special group? Yes, I do. I rejoice that there remain in the world ambitious and confident people with a strength of character, and the determination to succeed. You are taking your career seriously enough to put yourself through the hard-headed process of learning a difficult profession in a time when, as a rule, achievement and success are vilified. I find your drive to excel remarkable in respect to how unpopular it is.

I welcome you to the club, even at this early stage in your career. The courage to take that first step is often the most difficult aspect of the journey. You are welcome here. I pledge to share all I know, that it may help you succeed in one of the most difficult professions there is.

Sales is not difficult because it is hard or torturous. Sales is difficult because of many sellers' preconceived ideas about how to sell.

THE UNTRAINED SALESPERSON WILL GET HIS OR HER NOSE BLOODIED BY DEFENSIVE BUYERS WHO JUST WANT TO BE LEFT ALONE, OR WORSE, HAVE AN INHERENT DISLIKE FOR SALESPEOPLE.

Unfortunately for buyers, the product or service does not float into their living room on its own and show off its features. The product or service cannot connect a feature with the buyer's needs. Until someone figures out how to create a product that does, it is up to sellers to do their job.

In my view, sales is the greatest profession in the world. Where else can you earn a 6-figure living simply by talking with people and helping them get what they want? What other profession allows you to control your time and manage your work as you see fit?

Although I believe in the prosperity of sales as a profession, I also know that the salesperson is the biggest **Built-in-Major-Objection** in any offering of a product or service. The professional seller knows how to bring up that huge objection and make it an important addition to the sales process. The amateur does not and fights the *salesman battle* throughout the sales process.

The *salesman battle* is the seller's efforts to penetrate the buyer's protective screen he or she erects to keep the seller at a distance.

Why is this book a fraction of the length of most other books on sales? This book is purposely brief. My editor would prefer a thicker volume, filled with ponderous prose. As a consumer of sales training and self-help books, I don't like wordy sales reference books. I want the author to get to the point and dispense with the soap box lectures, or his or her psychological perspective on sales.

I don't believe in prattling on just to increase my word count. If you want a wordy book, please purchase one of my fiction novels. I have been told they are surprisingly good. If you want a quick read that was written with a respect for your time and effort, this is the one for you.

This book is a launching pad for your career. The topics covered here are fundamental to the sales business. Before you veteran salespeople groan at the idea of starting over, understand that you are not starting over, even if you have been selling for years.

Every professional athlete on any sports team, league, or association attends a pre-season training camp. During training camp, the professional athlete works on the fundamentals of his or her sport. When questioned by reporters, the professional athlete doesn't denounce the work he or she invests in practicing the fundamentals of the sport. Rather, most interviews and news stories quote the professional athlete extolling the benefits of a successful training camp.

PROFESSIONAL SALES IS REMARKABLY SIMILAR TO PROFESSIONAL SPORTS. LIKE ATHLETIC SKILL, SALES ACUMEN IS A PERISHABLE SKILL. IF YOU DON'T PRACTICE, YOU WILL LOSE YOUR SHARPNESS.

I must confess that writing this book has improved my sales techniques. As I wrote, I realized that, like the pro athlete, I knew the basics but had stopped using some of them. Writing this book caused me to focus on the fundamentals of sales. I can assure you I am using the fundamentals now.

I want you to consider this book a reference to which you may refer at any time. The table of contents is clear and concise. You can easily locate and review a specific topic. The book is thin enough that you can carry it with you in a brief case or tote.

I again thank you for choosing me and my book. Your options are numerous, and I am flattered and heartened that you selected this book.

INTRODUCTION

WELCOME TO THE MOMENT WHEN YOUR sales career will change forever. National studies show that more than 90% of working salespeople have never cracked a book on sales techniques. Almost 98% have never attended any type of outside sales training, classes, or seminars. This isn't a one-off fact. Untrained sellers are the new norm. Your purchasing this book places you in the top 10% of all sales professionals working today. Congratulations!

THE HISTORY OF MODERN SALES

Selling was reinvented as a skilled position during a renaissance of sorts; an era which stretched from the 1960's through the 1980's. J. Douglass Edwards is considered the father of modern day selling. Every sales technique taught in every sales seminar and sales manual can be linked directly to J. Douglass Edwards' methodology.

What was it about Edwards' approach to sales that changed the salesman from an undesirable aspect of the sale, to a key component in the negotiation for goods and services?

Many sales trainers claim that sales is the art of persuasion. I agree that persuasion is a part of the total skillset which comprises a professional seller, but it is not effective if misused or abused.

In the early days of modern sales, persuasion skills were considered the most valued. Often, the *art or persuasion* was focused upon, independent of the tools that make the skill work.

At the beginning of my sales career, much of what I was taught in direct sales training courses had to do with positioning a presentation in a way that put a prospect in a corner. He or she had to play by the seller's rules or risk being a liar. The seller depended upon the buyer's sense of honor and fair play to prevail.

Did it work? Sure, it did. Even poorly practiced sales techniques are more effective than a lack of technique. Back then there were no online reviews or social media with which to expose the tricksters. However, despite the information-sharing limitations of the day, the word got out that salespeople were manipulative and sneaky.

Over time, professional sales techniques – as they were believed to be – became unpopular with buyers and sellers. As the consumer became more sophisticated and better informed, clever sales tactics were shunned for fear of offending the buyer.

Hollywood bastardized modern sales techniques to fit an unattractive stereotype. Movies like *Tin Men*, *Glengarry Glen Ross*, *Cadillac Man*, and *Used Cars* portrayed salespeople as desperate and greedy con men, using trickery and subterfuge to take advantage of the unsuspecting buyer.

J. Douglass Edwards' groundbreaking sales transformation was taken out of context and rendered unpopular. Professional sales tactics were perceived as high pressure and pushy.

Since then, the fear of offending the most highly informed buyer of all time has relegated salespeople to walking product brochures and prolific proposers.

The State of Sales in the Heart of Free Enterprise

Like those terrified sellers who make up the majority of salespeople today, I believe that high pressure selling is a sin. There is no place in professional sales for pushy sellers. High pressure sales is the result of the clumsy implementation of sales techniques.

WHAT IS IT ABOUT A SELLER'S EFFORTS TO EARN A SALE THAT ARE PERCEIVED BY THE BUYER TO BE HIGH PRESSURE?

To earn a sale, the seller must generate **Sales Momentum**. This momentum appears in many forms, but generally it is an overall eagerness for the buyer to purchase a product or service from the seller. Sales Momentum must occur naturally. It must be organic to the relationship between the seller and the buyer. If that momentum is manufactured and unnatural to the relationship, it is perceived as high pressure.

How does Sales Momentum occur naturally? Like any crop, it must be planted and cultivated by the seller. This phenomenon begins with the seller's first contact with the buyer. You will learn how to plant the seeds of Sales Momentum.

Like high pressure, hard closing is a thing of the past. I don't mean it died with Mr. Edwards. Rather, when used as it was designed, closing is a valuable tool. Like persuasion, closing was focused upon by poor sales trainers, molding it into the process as a tricky word game that seduced salespeople with powerful persuasion tools and clever turns of phrase. The close was presented to sales trainees as verbal sleight of hand: verbal trickery wielded deftly by the sales magician.

The close is only as effective as the strength of the presentation. If you present an inch, you will have to close a mile. If you present a mile, you need only to close an inch.

Today, although the economy is stronger than it has ever been, the sales cycle is longer than ever, and more sales are lost to the lowest price. This is a remarkable travesty. Price should be the least concern for a buyer in a booming economy.

Sellers play the sales numbers as always. The numbers they play now, however, carry similar odds to those which determine the winners of the state lottery. Without an understanding of why a customer buys, the seller will never achieve sustainable sales statistics. The amount of time and effort required for the average modern seller to close a sale has been unnecessarily lengthened because of ignorance and misplaced fear.

THE CUSTOMER IS ALWAYS RIGHT

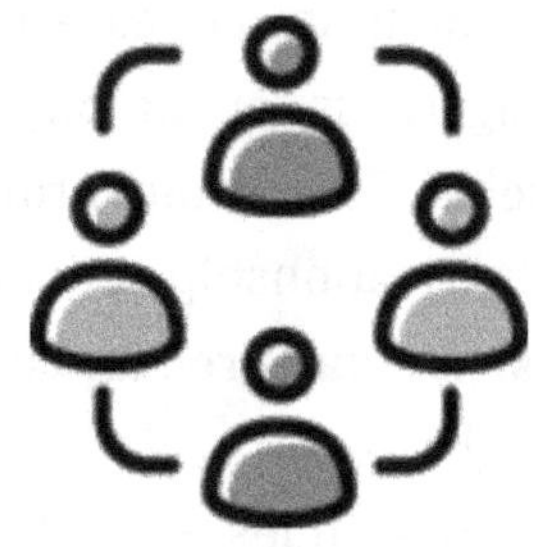

The saying *The Customer is Always Right* has never been taken more literally than it is today. The customer is not always right. If that were true, then anytime a customer says that a company, product, or service is horrible or overpriced, the company or product must necessarily be completely renovated or removed from the market. In the world of the customer is always right, when a customer tells you that your offer is too expensive, it means you must lower the price.

The customer is rarely right. The saying, *The Customer is Always Right* was the brainchild of the uninspired and overly altruistic mind of an unrealistic consumer advocate.

In a moment of brilliance, sales trainers recently conceived a creative correction to the misstatement. It is now said that the seller's job is to *Make the Customer be Right.*

My belief is less poetic but more practical than that. I believe that the seller's role is to:

BRING THE CUSTOMER INTO A STATE OF AGREEMENT WHERE THE PRODUCT OR SERVICE THE SELLER OFFERS MEETS THE BUYER'S NEEDS AND IS PRICED FAIRLY FOR WHAT IT PROVIDES IN USE AND QUALITY.

THE PATH OF LEAST RESISTANCE

Why do salespeople choose the path of least resistance, even at the risk of their income?

FEAR

Whether we fear rejection, or we fear confrontation, we all dislike being placed in a position where something we dread may occur.

A seller's fear is as real and unavoidable as the buyer's resentment of pressure. It is also as easily remedied. If the seller **Sets the Table for the Sales Process**, positioning himself or herself as a key component in the proposal presentation decision phase, the buyer will expect the seller's participation. The buyer will feel no resentment or fear in the seller providing that participation.

Many salespeople fail to earn the credibility required to be accepted by the buyer and are subsequently unwelcome beyond the delivery of the proposal.

With the prevalence of fearful salespeople today, buyers pick up on the fear of the seller and perceive any assertiveness by the seller as pressure. The buyer will welcome the lack of pressure in the seller's reluctance, and the sale will go to someone who is unafraid.

Applied to another profession, the reluctant seller is like a surgeon who is afraid to cut into a patient. In both cases, the buyer and the patient will suffer ill effect from the seller or surgeon's fears.

The path of least resistance is paved by fear. Find courage in the sales process. The process works.

YOUR ROLE AS A PROFESSIONAL SELLER

It is not necessary that you become an expert on the product or service you offer. In many cases your technical knowledge can confuse a buyer who knows little about the nuts and bolts of your product and may create unhelpful objections.

Often, sellers fall back upon their technical knowledge as a crutch rather than depending upon the sales process to deliver them the sale.

I spent much of my career in the home improvement sales business. Most "salespeople" in the remodeling industry are former business owners and tradespeople.

I agree that industry knowledge in as technically demanding a business as remodeling is helpful, but I believe equally that most of that knowledge is unnecessary with the use of skillful selling techniques.

It is rare that a highly trained technician or a former trades person is also good at professional sales. Conversely, it is just as rare that a professional career seller is also adept at the technical or mechanical aspects of his or her product or service.

The skills to be a technical person are much different than those which comprise a professional seller. The personalities of the two vocations often vary widely. The chances that the proper personality and aptitude for each vocation meet in one person is remote.

It is more practical to train a professional seller in the features and benefits of a product or service than it is to train a technician or artisan how to sell at a professional level.

Professional selling requires little more than a cursory understanding of a product or service. A technician, however, would have to completely educate himself or herself in the complexities of the sales process to sell his or her product or service effectively.

As I mentioned, most salespeople in the remodeling industry are construction experts and current or former construction business owners.

MOST CONFUSE THEIR EXPERIENCE WITH SALES ABILITY.

These builder salespeople are godsends for the remodeling buyer. The unknowledgeable buyer will glean much industry insight from these experts. Unfortunately for the technician salesperson, his or her construction expertise serves only to provide the buyer free advice and knowledge, and the sale ultimately goes to a salesperson with the ability to execute an effective sales process. Even the detailed information contained within the construction expert's emailed proposal helps the buyer to purchase from a different company.

As a professional seller, you will be a treasured asset to any company. Ironically, because of the rarity of skilled salespeople today, your unusual success may seem like luck or some type of subterfuge to your colleagues. To ownership and management, at first your success may be suspect considering the lack of results they have seen from those salespeople with whom you work.

I worked with a remodeling company that relied upon bidding for sales generation. When in my first three weeks I sold $182,000.00 in gross volume, the ownership and management grew suspicious of my unprecedented sales numbers. They suspected I had made mistakes in my project estimates and the buyers had snatched up the low offers.

After a considerable period of reviewing the proposals and the project sites, the ownership and management concluded that the new sales were accurately priced and contained large margins.

I never grew angry or frustrated with the owners and managers. I knew innately that what I had done in a very few weeks had never been done before in their company. Where they sold based upon a multi-week or, more typically, a multi-month sales cycle, I sold based upon a 7 to 14-day sales cycle.

The more the trend towards professional selling grows, the happier sellers and their customers will be.

IF 5-STAR RATINGS ARE IMPORTANT TO YOUR BUSINESS, UNDERSTAND THAT A WELL-TRAINED,

HIGHLY PRODUCING SALES STAFF WILL LEAD TO CUSTOMER SATISFACTION.

I was a member of another sales team where I saw displayed the trappings of a sales force. The walls were adorned with catchy slogans like *Acme's Sales Team Rocks, Success is only a Sale Away, Hang in there, it's almost Friday.* That was where the similarity to a professional sales organization ended.

The sales meetings focused on the availability of leads and ways of being prolific at generating proposals. The sales team's combined closing percentage was around 10%. A certain number of proposals were expected to be tendered each month. Management tracked the sales numbers accordingly.

When I learned this, I asked the sales manager, "What makes you more money, proposals or sales?

"Both, "the sales manager replied.

A proposal has never made anyone a dime. Sales make you money.

The fight against sales techniques is real. Most sales organizations would rather lose a sale than use what they believe to be high-pressure tactics.

As I have shared with you, high pressure is the stock and trade of the aggressive amateur. Asking for the sale is an art form. Sales professionals know this and refine their skills in using it.

One sales organization of which I was a part, refused to post monthly sales numbers on the sales board. It was believed that the practice was confrontational and demeaning. The company management and ownership believed it was wrong to compare performance data amongst the salespeople. The company owners and management believed salespeople should not compete with one another. They are a team.

Why would a sales organization refuse to post individual sales numbers when the metric for success is total annual revenue? Could it be for the same reason it is considered inappropriate to ask a buyer for his or her business today?

The reason is clear to me. We have grown up in a society where everyone gets a trophy, not just the champs. Teachers routinely ask the ultimate anti-capitalist question when a student is chewing gum. *Did you bring enough gum for the whole class?*

The same could be asked about her paycheck. *Did you get paid enough for the whole class?* Individual effort and accomplishment are never popular in today's society. Achievement is no longer a goal nor is it recognized or rewarded.

Co-workers are taught they are part of a team. If that were true, wouldn't the team structure include team members ponying up part of their salary to help out the teammate who was having a hard time paying his or her debts?

Ultimately, we are alone, and personally responsible for our success or failure. The team mentality is a mechanism designed to distribute the pain of failure to the entire group rather than focusing it upon the individual member. In this team mentality, success also is necessarily distributed within the team rather than focusing attention upon the stand-out member. If there is a winner, there must necessarily be a loser. Today, the individual impact is too confrontational and thus unacceptable.

A business owner told me once that money isn't the most important thing. Maybe not, but philanthropy is not a booming business, and few businesses are founded solely to benefit the customer.

SAYING "MONEY IS NOT THE MOST IMPORTANT THING" SEEMS COMPASSIONATE, BUT IT DOES NO MORE THAN VIRTUE SIGNAL THE MESSAGE, "I DON'T WANT TO BE THOUGHT OF AS A GREEDY CAPITALIST."

If you prefer to use the term greed rather than success, then greed is the driving force behind capitalism. Many who embrace a Keynesian economic model view profit as a bad thing. I believe that ambition drives commerce and benefits anyone with whom it comes in contact.

When an entrepreneurial businessperson founds a company, he or she will necessarily create jobs to produce a product or service, sell, and distribute that product or service. Jobs are created with the company's vendors and suppliers as goods and services are purchased for provisioning and supplying the endeavor. In short, the greed/ambition of a single person benefits many.

An extraordinarily successful businessman, and a friend of mine, explained profit to me. I think his opinion is accurate.

"A SALARY IS WHAT A BUSINESSMAN PAYS HIMSELF TO RUN A BUSINESS. PROFIT IS WHAT HE PAYS HIMSELF FOR THE RISK HE ASSUMES WHILE RUNNING A BUSINESS."

If you are a commissioned sales professional, a large component of your vocation is competition. Whether the competition is another company or another seller, the prize for being the best is more money and a better life for you and your loved ones. You have a right to success. Success is elusive for those who never learn the basics of sales. The key to being successful is to work diligently in an effective way.

The most difficult part of a sales career is the beginning. The fear of relying upon the uncertainty of a commission income works on you. Most novice salespeople are undercapitalized, and the desperation for a paycheck is a palpable thing that the buyer will perceive as a distraction to the sales process.

One of my early sales managers recognized the desperation of the new salesperson in me. I never talked about my personal life, but he knew just the same.

I was in the one-call-close, home improvement sales business. I was provided 3 appointments per day. Many of them were hundreds of miles from my home and office. All my expenses were on me. There was no guarantee I would sell the lead once I arrived. Many times, the prospects *Dark-Housed* me. That is the industry term for the homeowner leaving the home before the appointment to avoid the salesman.

My wife was not happy with my new profession. She disliked the long hours and the possibility of no paycheck on payday. Her worries were justified, which made the job harder for me to stick with.

One day the sales manager asked me to remain after the sales meeting. When we were alone, he asked me how things were going at home.

I told him everything was fine.

He nodded knowingly and this is what he said.

"Craig, when you go into a customer's home and you are worried about your bills or about your family, they can smell the desperation on you. You must check your problems at the door. Depend upon your sales presentation, and the quality of our products, and you will succeed."

I asked him, "How do I check my problems at the door?"

He replied:

"JUST GO OUT THERE AND PICK SH WITH THE CHICKENS EVERY DAY, AND THE MONEY WILL TAKE CARE OF ITSELF."**

From that day I found a way to focus on the work, and the money did take care of itself.

My goal is to show you that way. I don't want you to suffer as I did. My hope is that you benefit from the information in this book and join me as a Professional Seller.

[1]

Chapter 1 – Professional Selling

NO MATTER THE INDUSTRY, THE CUSTOMER'S needs are the same in respect to their relationship with the seller. It has been said by sales trainers of the past, that the customer buys you and what you are doing, and you give them the product for free. Although the saying is more clever than it is accurate, the message is sound. A buyer will not purchase from someone he or she doesn't like and trust.

Warm regard from a buyer is not a guarantee of the sale, but dislike and indifference will guarantee a lost sale.

How do you earn the buyer's favor?

Get to know the buyer and, more importantly, let them get to know you. As a professional seller, you must define the terms of your relationship with the buyer. You must position the relationship as one of professional mutual interest, based upon a mutual benefit.

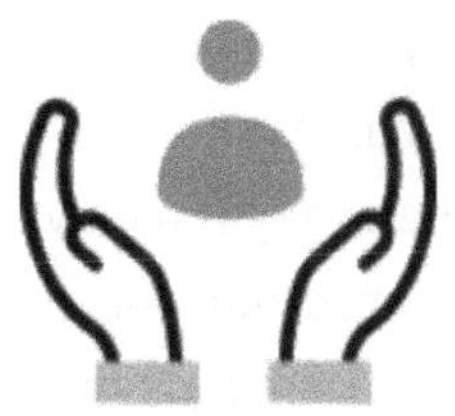

Limit your personal investment of information and intimacy to only those things that will add to that mutual benefit as it applies to the sale.

The time to develop rapport is during the **Warmup Q&A** phase, as you **Set the Table for the Sales Process**. We will cover setting the table for the sales process as this chapter progresses.

Why Must We Focus on the Fundamentals?

At its highest levels, selling is a remarkably technical vocation. Much of what we do is based upon proper training and grueling repetition. To a great degree, our intuition grows stronger with experience. Intuition is a valuable tool in deciphering the fears and motivations of the buyer.

To achieve a high level of understanding of our customers, we sellers must use our sales skills effectively. Our experiences, drawn from the buyer's reactions to our sales tools, help us refine our selling intuition.

I hear it often said that today buyers are more knowledgeable and better informed than at any other time in history. With access to unlimited information via the web and social media, consumers have figured out the sales game. Sellers are no longer needed for buyers to acquire goods or services.

Those same observations were made in the eighties when I began my sales career. I agree that today information is the most available it has ever been. I also agree that consumers are better informed than they have ever been. I reject that consumers have salespeople figured out and that sellers are no longer needed for the buyer to acquire goods or services.

No one is an expert on everything. We all need help from others. Professional sellers bring a timeless need to any buyer's trek from not having something to buying something.

Most salespeople have surrendered to the preconceptions bandied about, portraying sellers as grifters and con men. The critics have no clue what they are talking about. Selling is in many ways a philanthropic pursuit.

At a casual glance, you may believe that philanthropy is rarely associated with profitability. Is it? The medical field is dedicated almost purely to philanthropy. Doctors are amongst the highest paid professionals in our society.

Sellers make the buying process easier. Those who are most effective are rewarded generously because of the skill required to earn a sale despite fierce competition and preconceived negatives.

The skilled sales professional achieves remarkable closing numbers with regularity. Those elite few are the best at what they do. With rarity comes value. With value comes a hefty price tag.

SALES IS THE HIGHEST PAID PROFESSION, LEAVING DOCTORS AND ATTORNEYS BEHIND BY A LARGE MARGIN.

A highly skilled seller will make the single most significant contribution to a company's success. There is no other aspect or component of the business which can compare.

Do you want to achieve the acclaim and profitability of the elite seller? If you focus on the fundamentals you will make a comfortable living in sales as your experience grows. With that experience, you will gain insight into the workings of the buyer's mind. Your selling intuition will develop and selling will become easy for you.

I don't recall the exact date I became a member of the elite. I know that at a point, sales became easy for me. When that happened, I became the consistently highest producing seller on any sales team within which I worked.

Learn the fundamentals of the profession of sales and you will never worry about your next paycheck. You will be rendered recession proof. You will always be in demand.

Do Buyers Purchase Emotionally or Logically?

The heated debate on the subject has fueled sales training seminars for years. Some believe the sale is made completely emotionally. Others tout the hard-working Purchasing Manager as the best example of buying logically. Wishy-washy-feel-gooders believe that emotion must be weaved into the buyer's logical screen. The result is that the buyer moves into a state of agreement with the seller, thus connecting with him or her emotionally.

Here is the controversial answer:

NONE OF THE ABOVE.

For the credible sales professional, sales is a process of appealing to the buyer's sense of loyalty.

We have all heard the left-handed compliment, "He could sell ice cubes to an Eskimo."

The saying is insulting to a professional seller because the transaction between seller and Eskimo is based upon misplaced trust.

As professional sellers, it is our sacred obligation to help the buyer decide on the best product or service for his or her needs or desires, based upon honest fact-finding, and sincere interest and concern for the buyer.

If you believe customers make buying decisions emotionally, and craft your presentation to suit that belief, you will sell only to impulsive, irresponsible money squandering buyers.

If you sell strictly logically, you are no more than a proposer and order-taker. Your success will depend upon being the lowest bidder.

If you believe that you must manipulate the buyer with a psychological process which brings him or her into agreement with you, then you will make many friends but earn few sales.

The sales process invests the buyer with confidence in the seller. This confidence comes from the seller's credibility and perceived motivations. The buyer will always pay extra for peace of mind. The buyer will always pay a bit more to someone he or she trusts and likes. The buyer wants to perceive value from the product. The buyer wants to be treated fairly and truthfully.

Technical Experts vs Sales Professionals

Some years ago, I worked with a large remodeling company. The firm had invested a lot of capital in new offices, company trucks, and office staff as they opened a market in a new town.

I answered an ad requesting applications from experienced salespeople. At the interview, the sales manager bragged that he had filled all the sales positions except the one for which I had applied. As he continued telling me about the company and how the sales staff was expected to work, he confessed sadly that he had a background in timeshare sales and had little experience in the construction industry. He vouchsafed that he hoped to learn from his new sales force.

I told him that I was surprised that he had been able to hire so many sales professionals in such a short period of time. Remodeling sales is an advanced, executive sales position, selling a technically complex, big-ticket item. From experience I knew that, even in a large city, there were few sellers with the experience and sales skill necessary to sell such a challenging service.

He assured me that he had found the most construction knowledgeable candidates available.

With pride he said, "All of them are former project managers and construction experts."

Over the next few months his new sales team fell well short of the numbers expected by corporate. The manager lost his job and I replaced him.

I immediately changed the hiring criteria, and gradually replaced the technical salespeople with professional sellers.

As I wrote earlier in the book:

IT IS MUCH EASIER TO TEACH A PROFESSIONAL SELLER AN ADEQUATE TECHNICAL SKILL NECESSARY TO SELL A PRODUCT EFFECTIVELY, THAN IT IS TO TEACH AN ARTISAN OR A TRADESMAN PROFESSIONAL SALES.

Early in my career I joined an upstart telecom company as sales manager and marketing director. The founder and owner of the company was a technician. His life was his new *Class 5 switch*. He knew everything about the technical aspects of telecommunications. He could tell you anything you wanted to know about *T-1's, twisted pairs, Co-Lo centers and Time Division Multiplexing.*

He and I made a sales call on the vice president of a large bank downtown. The bank executive asked how the call worked. My boss, the technician company owner, took a deep breath and began a highly technical explanation of how a call processor picked up the call and routed it to the switch where it travelled across a 24 channel T-1 , blah, blah, blah.

I watched as the executive's eyes glazed and he sagged in his expensive leather chair.

I used a control phrase to stop my boss' technical monologue and said simply, "You punch this button on your phone, and when you hear the fast busy, you dial the number."

The banker nodded his understanding, and we earned his business that day.

I understood the banker's question to be a **Buying Signal**. My instinct was to qualify the question and close the sale. As a professional seller, I have been trained to do so.

When a technician receives a question, he or she will instinctively provide an informative and complex reply.

SALES IS EVERY BIT THE EDUCATIONALLY-BASED PURSUIT OF ANY WHITE-COLLAR CAREER.

Doctors, Attorneys, and Teachers spend years acquiring their credentials and the skills necessary to perform their jobs at a professional level. Sales is an advanced executive pursuit requiring a commensurate education and skill. Despite the need for training in the skills of professional sales, most salespeople believe they can succeed without it because they possess the technical knowledge of their product or service.

There were no training manuals on driving nails or repairing cars in the sales section where you purchased this book. Your sales acumen provides more value to the buyer than your technical knowledge ever will.

Be Informative, But Never Reveal Proprietary Materials

Have you ever watched any of those real estate broker reality shows? I reluctantly admit that recently I watched one of them.

On the screen, a well-dressed real estate broker chatted with a hugely successful property owner about representing him to sell three units of his multi-million-dollar property in New York.

The owner asked the broker how he planned to make the property stand out in the market.

Unbelievably, the realtor crossed his arms and said the following to the property owner:

"I won't tell you about my ideas until you have signed up with me. If I do, you will take my ideas and give them to another broker to use."

I watched the property owner in the coverage of the scene. Although he was aware that he was on TV, and he was following the directions of the production staff, he exhibited all of the non-verbal signs of annoyance and discomfort any buyer would at the insulting accusations of the seller.

The property owner even quartered his stance away from the real estate agent and moved to where the kitchen island was between he and the seller.

After delivering this insensitive remark, the broker stood there, looking at the owner.

I can only presume that the director said, "Pick up your cues," because after a long uncomfortable pause, the property owner broke into a big smile and extended his hand to the broker.

"Let's do it," he said, and they shook hands.

In the real world, the multi-millionaire property owner would have immediately tossed the insulting salesperson out of the building.

If he were unnaturally forgiving, and didn't immediately call security, the property owner would never buy from a seller who first insulted him, accusing him of being unscrupulous, then didn't bother to ask for his business.

As sellers, we often fear that our proposals, drawings, proprietary company information, and even our pricing might be used by a competitor to earn the sale. Would a buyer stoop to doing something so unscrupulous? Of course there are those who would.

I believe that we must never leave proprietary materials with a non-customer. I also as strongly believe that you should never share your concerns with a buyer in that way. If I were the broker, I might have handled it this way.

"Mr. Owner, I have some great ideas that will make your property shine in the market. When you become my client, I will share a detailed plan with you to do just that. Where do you want me to send the contract?"

Components of the Buyer / Seller Relationship

Much of the guilt amateur salespeople feel at selling to a buyer stems from a false sense of intrusion. Many sellers feel like they are imposing upon the buyer, and uncomfortable in their selfish pursuit of the sale. Before your own guilt taints your judgement, let's examine the buyer and his or her motivation to meet with a salesperson.

Why is the Seller Meeting with the Buyer?

In the sales relationship, the seller is often an invited guest to the buyer's home or business. Most of us generate our leads from lead services or from requests for bids. The buyer asks the seller to visit, or the buyer comes to the seller's office or showroom. The buyer is not coerced into the appointment by the seller.

Why is the Seller Meeting with the Buyer about the Product?

The product or service the seller offers is something the buyer wants or needs. The buyer proactively embarked upon an uncomfortable journey to acquire the seller's product or service. The experience violates the buyer's innate defense mechanisms, but he or she ignores the discomfort in order to obtain the product or service he or she desires.

Why Does the Seller Need to be a Part of the Sale?

Professional sellers fulfill a role for the buyer. If a seller is necessary enough to the sale that the buyer cannot purchase the product or service by walking into a store or ordering it online, the seller is an advocate and professional liaison between the buyer's needs and the product or service's features and benefits.

WHY SHOULD THE BUYER WANT TO BUY TODAY?

When buyers tell professional sellers that they would never buy from a pushy salesperson today, what they are saying is that they would never buy from an amateur. Helping the buyer to make a buying decision ends an uncomfortable process and alleviates the anguish of making a decision. Every sale results in gratitude and relief for the buyer.

SALES MANAGER REHASH – BE CAREFUL

In sales, many sales managers conduct a **Rehash** of lost sales or unsuccessful sales presentations. One of the sales managers who conducted a Sales Rehash with me was not a professional salesperson. The sales manager was more of an administrator than a seller. As such, the sales manager understood little about the sales process.

After I gave my recounting of the sales presentation, the manager made a personal observation. He told me that my tactics were too pushy. He told me that he would never buy from anyone who sold like I do.

I explained that I had recounted the particulars of the sale in bullet form. The customer's experience was much more detailed and would require a lot of time to repeat. I assured the manager that because he had seen behind the curtain, the magic was no longer a mystery.

The sales process is successful only when the tools are used in harmony and completely. Taken piece by piece, the tools of the professional seller can appear to be tricky or ineffective. I assured him that he would buy from a professional who sold properly, using an effective sales process.

The sales manager rejected my assertion without further comment. Frustrated with the sales manager's dogged resistance, I asked him if any of the sales I had made that month had resulted in the buyer complaining about my being pushy or high pressure.

He admitted that they had not. He did, however, hint that some of the buyers who had not purchased from me mentioned, in the *Customer Follow-up Review,* that I had seemed pushy.

I asked for specific cases. He told me that he would have to review his notes and get back to me. He never got back to me.

My request for the specific cases was not intended to defend my sales techniques or to shift blame. I expect lost sales to return bad reviews about my techniques. Many times, bad reviews indicate a quality performance on the seller's part.

We don't get every sale, but the rehash will reveal whether or not we followed the sales process despite the lost sale.

IF THE SELLER IS SKILLED AT THE SALES PROCESS, HE OR SHE WILL DEVELOP A RELATIONSHIP WITH THE BUYER.

The reason you always ask for the sale, is to take the buyer / seller relationship to the next logical level. If the buyer rejects the invitation to go to the next level, there is a breakdown in the relationship.

Many of us have experienced the heartache of divorce or have been jilted by someone we loved. Every broken relationship begins with love and passion. Husbands and wives enter marriage with the highest ideals and the optimism only true love can inspire.

When the relationship fails, the hearts and flowers disappear. There is always a heavy dose of blame flung at the other. Sometimes the blame is warranted, other times it is a justification or excuse for the guilt of failing in the relationship.

Sales is no different. When the seller sets the table for the sales process, he or she enters a relationship with the buyer. Whether it works out and a sale is made, or it fails, and the sale is lost, the relationship is affected.

If the seller has done well, regardless of earning the sale or not, there will be an emotional investment by both parties. When that investment bears fruit, everyone sings, and smiles beam from all sides. When that investment fails, there will be hard feelings.

A seller/buyer relationship is not invested as deeply as a love relationship, so the stakes are not as high. The resulting hurt feelings are commensurately less painful.

A lack of negative feedback from the buyer during a rehash indicates there a relationship was never established. It is a bigger mistake to avoid the relationship piece in order to avoid a bad rehash, than it is to lose a sale and suffer a poor review as a result of the hurt feelings of a lost relationship.

[2]

Chapter 2 – Setting the Table for the Sales Process

FROM THE FIRST MOMENT YOU meet with the buyer, whether it is in person or on the phone, you are **Setting the Table for the Sales Process**. Part of your work includes establishing a good first impression, but much of it is spent conditioning the buyer to your role in the sales process. It is crucial that you, as a seller, create a role where you are a critically important component in the buyer's decision-making efforts.

Most salespeople plant seeds of low expectations during the first contact with the buyer. Many assume an air of apologetic meekness. The guilt sellers feel at taking up the buyer's time while try to earn a sale dominates the interview.

Many salespeople attempt to alleviate their discomfort by attempting to create a personal relationship with the buyer in order to gain favor. As we will discuss in the **Fish on the Wall** section, this is a grave error.

As sellers, we battle our instinctive urge to side with the buyer against us. Although this seems counter-intuitive, we must recognize that our human nature moves us as it does the buyer. The buyer's instinct to resist the seller is called the **Buyer Defense Mechanism**.

Sellers Root for the Buyer

As sellers, we instinctively root for the buyer. The professional seller understands this instinct, and resists the urge to side with the buyer.

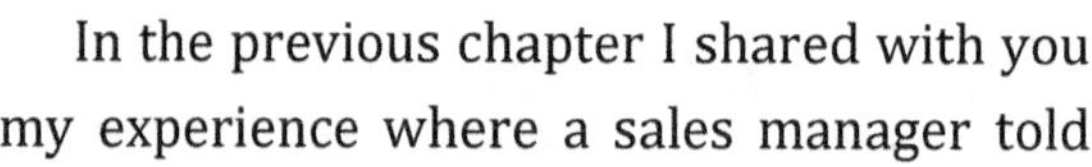

In the previous chapter I shared with you my experience where a sales manager told me that he would never buy from anyone who sold like I do. He said he would never fall for the tricks I use as a salesman.

When I remarked that everyone, including salespeople, root for the buyer, even to their detriment as a seller, he rejected the premise.

The sales manager was remarkably knowledgeable about the industry, but he had apparently never been trained in the art of professional selling.

Because the relationship between us had exposed him to only a summary knowledge of what I knew, he naturally distrusted my methods and perceived them as tricks and gimmicks.

> **TO THE AMATEUR SELLER, ASKING FOR THE SALE; ASKING FOR COMMITMENTS FROM THE BUYER; AND ASKING FOR THE ORDER TODAY, IS UNPLEASANT AND PUSHY.**

The sales manager finally said, "I would never buy from a pushy, high pressure salesman. I have been treated that way and I won't tolerate it."

I was the new salesman on the team. Interestingly, I had sold more in my first month than the entire sales team combined. The management and ownership were suspicious of my sales success because they had never seen it done before.

That company's sales team relied upon a proposal process where they had to be the lowest bidder to sell their service.

No one had trained them to **Set the Table for the Sales Process**. None of them tried to close the business. They habitually emailed proposals. Their admitted closing percentage hovered around 7 - 10%.

Why do amateurs Side with the Buyer?

Even my resistant sales manager buys from professional sellers. His bad experiences occurred at the hands of rank amateurs and order takers. Because he, and so many like him, believe that salespeople are innately selfish and distrustful, they conduct themselves as sellers as if it were true about them too.

Let me remind you why customers buy more often from professional sellers than amateur order takers. Many salespeople consider what they do to be invasive and confrontational. The belief that they would never buy from a seller who pressed for the business comes from seeing behind the curtain, so to speak. The amateur seller views the sales process from the perspective of the **Buyer Defense Mechanism.** Combined with an inherent guilt at wanting the sale, the amateur feels he or she is taking advantage of a buyer in need.

Conversely, the Professional Seller understands and values the need for the service he or she provides. The buyer opposes salespeople because of a preconceived notion that salespeople are innately devious and distrustful. The Professional Seller is neither devious nor distrustful. The Professional Seller holds critical industry insight and understanding of how a product or service will fit with the buyer's needs.

The Buyer Defense Mechanism

Never sell the way you like to buy! Human nature has allowed for an array of protective measures that ensure a buyer will avoid making any kind of decision which may result in discomfort or pain. We call this the **Buyer Defense Mechanism.**

NEVER SELL THE WAY YOU LIKE TO BUY.

We are sellers and we recognize the Buyer Defense Mechanism in our prospects' resistance to our attempts to sell. Despite knowing about it, when we sellers buy a product or service, our own Buyer Defense Mechanism engages. We resist the very thing we do for a living. Although we are aware of why we react to a seller as we do, the natural instinct to defend ourselves engages, nonetheless.

Do Sellers Need to Evolve?

I read an online article, written by a non-salesperson, who warned of the dangers of pressuring buyers in the sales process. His article was inspired by a poll taken amongst buyers of sold-in-home services. The author claimed that, unanimously, the study subjects believed that sellers *Need to Evolve*. The poll participants complained that modern salespeople are "pushy." Part of the online poll included an opportunity for those buyers to offer advice to salespeople on how they might improve their sales processes.

THE LAST PERSON YOU WANT TO CONSULT FOR SALES ADVICE IS A BUYER.

The buyer's perceptions come from the **Buyer Defense Mechanism**. Unbelievably, most salespeople predicate their selling techniques upon what the Buyer Defense Mechanism defines as comfortable, and employ only those tactics that cause the buyer the least discomfort.

The same study found that 80% of all sales required five or more follow-ups in order to close. That statistical claim is staggering in how it represents the ineptitude of modern salespeople.

Is it any wonder that these customers think salespeople are pushy when they follow-up five more times after the proposal has been tendered?

How can a seller justify so many call-backs? What delaying condition could the buyer present to the seller that would require five attempts before making a decision?

Salespeople habitually email and text crucial information to their prospects. Even proposals and contracts are delivered digitally for approval. This is an accommodating arrangement if you are a buyer avoiding a buying decision, or you are a salesperson who dislikes contact with others. Is it a good idea if you want to make a living as a seller?

NO!

Proposals and contracts are documents only. They wield no magical sales ability.

I was in a sales meeting where the sales manager asked the members of the sales team if they believed it was better to email a proposal, or to deliver it in person.

Several of the salespeople answered that they preferred emailing them because it took the pressure off the seller.

One salesman observed that the husband and wife would want to talk over the proposal and could not do so if the salesperson was present.

I was intrigued at the observation and asked the salesman a question:

"The proposal contains technical and proprietary information unique to the industry," I said. "Other than price, what could the husband and wife discuss that they would not need the seller present to explain?"

The salesman had no reply. He grew angry and defensive. He had spoken from the perspective of his **Buyer Defense Mechanism**. He could produce no reasonable explanation for his ill-conceived opinion.

Finally, in frustration, he told me that he didn't buy that way and he would not high pressure his customers that way.

This salesman had no problem aggressively displaying to me his assertiveness in defense of his mistaken belief that emailing the proposal is better. If he employed half of that passion towards helping the buyer own his product or service, his sales numbers would be impressive indeed.

Overcoming The Buyer Defense Mechanism

The greatest obstacle to the sale is the battle against human nature. It is unfortunate, but no one likes a salesman. Even salespeople dislike salespeople.

In sales, much time and effort are invested in overcoming the **Buyer Defense Mechanism**. This is the reason so many sales training books delve into the customer's psyche, searching for a psychological trigger with which to handle the buyer's resistance to the seller. It may surprise many salespeople to know that the most effective method of defeating the Buyer Defense Mechanism is not an exercise in psychology.

May I Help You?

The most common manifestation of the Buyer Defense Mechanism occurs in retail, during the first contact between buyer and seller.

"Good morning", the seller says to an arriving customer. "Can I help you?"

The reply is immediate and automatic. "No thanks. I'm just looking."

Imagine this: You have planned for months to purchase a new TV. You have saved, and with your most recent commission check, you finally have the money together to purchase your TV.

You have researched web sources online during those months of saving, weighing your buying options. You have finally settled upon one of two models.

You drive to the big national retail chain store and enter the building. The first person you see asks to help you buy the TV you have planned to purchase for months and you tell him or her "No thanks, I'm just looking."

After rejecting the first salesperson's offer to help you, you make your way to the back of the store where flickering images beckon from TV's along the back wall. You look at the TV's until you locate the two you are considering.

A different salesperson in a logo golf shirt approaches you.

"Can I help you find something?" he asks meekly.

You feel a rising discomfort, but you accept his offer to help.

"I am interested in buying one of these TV's," you say. "I'm not sure whether I should go with the Samsung or the LG."

The salesman begins a product comparison based upon features and costs.

Because you have done your homework, you feel resentment and impatience, but you listen. Gradually you become more comfortable, and ultimately the salesperson helps you decide on a TV.

Why is it that a professional seller feels exactly as any buyer feels about salespeople? Even when you have planned to purchase, have money in hand, and drove to the store specifically to buy, you still resent the salesperson's participation. Only after the seller has spent time providing you the assistance you needed and wanted, do you grow comfortable with him or her.

Human nature controls our innate reactions. Our Buyer Defense Mechanism is as real as a fear of heights, spiders, or strangers. The intrusion of a salesman falls under the stranger danger category. That instinct, coupled with the risk of being tricked out of your money, relegates the salesperson's presence to one of danger - albeit a low category of danger.

Credibility – The Backbone of the Sale

The most important aspect of the sales process is the seller's **Credibility**. The seller's leadership and insight lend direction and structure to the sales process.

Often, your customers have never purchased what you sell. Their knowledge of your industry may be limited to what they have seen on TV or online. Likely, much of what they know is frightening to them, warranted or not. Your first task is to develop the rapport of a knowledgeable and caring advocate to a reluctantly trusting novice.

CREDIBILITY IS THE FEATURE OF YOUR SALES PROCESS THAT MEANS THE MOST TO THE BUYER.

Positioning yourself as a reliable and trustworthy fixture in the sales process is the single most important goal when **Setting the Table for the Sales Process**.

If you present yourself as a kindly information gatherer who will assemble a proposal with which the buyer can compare other bids, your role in the sales process ends once the proposal is delivered.

This is the reason many salespeople are perceived as pushy or high pressure. If the buyer's perception of you is that you are a proposer, you will be out of place if you try to encourage a decision after the proposal is delivered.

If you position yourself as a valuable resource for industry insight, pricing and product delivery, and a protection against unexpected trouble, you will have a welcome place at the table when the decision is being made.

If you don't create that role for yourself, the buyer will relegate your importance to that of a clerk or an estimator. You have value in the sales process. Don't cheat the buyer out of your assistance in buying your product or service.

How is Credibility Earned with the Buyer?

The best way to earn credibility is to ask questions which reveal concerns you and your product or service can be instrumental in eliminating.

Most buyers enter a sales interview with a preconceived notion of how the process will go. Initially, the buyer believes the seller is selfishly pursuing the sale. As such, his or her Buyer Defense Mechanism is on high alert and the buyer will present a resistant front to the seller. This front is often contrived and displayed as a particular emotion. Some buyers are grave and considering; others display an air of formal cordiality with an undertone of guarded caution.

If you don't change the buyer's emotional state, you will not earn his or her business. If the buyer is jovial, introduce a measure of sadness. If the buyer is stern or serious, introduce a lighter mood into the interview. If the buyer is confident or noncommittal, warn against dangers inherent in the industry for which your product or service provides a solution.

This transformation takes time to complete. The **Warm-up Q&A** is the time to build credibility and change the buyer's emotional state. The seller's credibility will grow as the buyer's front shrinks.

The Customer Buys You and What You are Doing

From the moment you enter the buyer's life, you are being evaluated. Everything about you, from how you dress, to how you express your thoughts and ideas are on trial. Remember, the salesperson is the largest **Built-in-Major-Objection** to any product or service. Although the seller plays only a temporary role in the buyer's relationship with a product or service, the buyer will make his or her buying decision, to a large degree, upon how he or she feels about the seller.

THE CUSTOMER BUYS YOU AND WHAT YOU ARE DOING. YOU GIVE THEM THE PRODUCT FOR FREE.

I find it fascinating how easily a buyer slips into the role of interviewer during a sales presentation. As consumers, when we spend money with a seller or a company, we expect to be treated as their better. For a moment, we have purchased the right to a higher station.

Studies have shown that buyers like to purchase from people they perceive as successful. Car dealerships act upon that premise when they tout being the number one dealership in the area. The manufacturer is the same and the vehicle normally is similarly priced. What difference does it make to a potential car buyer whether he or she buys from the top seller or from a lesser competitor?

PRESTIGE

J. Douglass Edwards devoted a huge portion of his training seminars to dressing for the sale. First impressions are indeed the most important. He would work himself into a lather on the dais, striking a fist into his palm, as he warned his students to arrive fifteen minutes early, dressed in a suit, ready to present the product or service perfectly.

During the days when I sold remodeling services, I learned that I was one of the few sellers who showed up in business attire. Arriving early for my appointments, many times I saw the competition leaving the home. Most were dressed in work boots and jeans. Sometimes they wore a logo tee or golf shirt. They climbed into their work trucks and drove away as I approached the home, dressed smartly, carrying my leather briefcase.

I never forgot that when I made a sales call, I was not in the construction business. I was in the sales business.

People like to spend time with successful interesting people. I advise any seller to dress and conduct himself or herself as such.

[3]

Chapter 3 – First Contact with the Buyer

Prospecting

Today, lead generation is rarely a part of the seller's responsibility unless the seller generates prospects via cold calling. Usually leads are purchased through a lead service, search engines, (SEO) optimized web sites, TV / Radio / Social Media advertising, mass mailers or door hangers.

If cold calling is your method, there are techniques you must know to penetrate the protective screen - the **Buyer Defense Mechanism** - with which businesses and homeowners surround themselves.

I spent much of my sales career in B2B sales. My preferred method of prospecting B2B, is *door knocking* or canvassing. When I share my preference for in-person cold calling, the dark reaction of immediate dismissal is a palpable thing among sales trainees.

Everyone dislikes and dreads cold calling.

Years ago, a top sales trainer announced in a clear and accusatorial tone to a crowded hall

"THE DIFFERENCE BETWEEN THE SUCCESSFUL PEOPLE IN THIS ROOM AND THE UNSUCCESSFUL PEOPLE IN THIS ROOM, IS THAT THE SUCCESSFUL PEOPLE MAKE A HABIT OF DOING THE THINGS THAT THE UNSUCCESSFUL PEOPLE AVOID."

I am a professional, but I don't like cold calling any more than you do. I do, however, like large commission checks and being the top salesman.

Have you noticed an emerging theme in this book? With so few professionals in the industry, you can and will be the top producer simply by doing a fraction more than everyone else is doing.

In sales – and life – a 1% greater effort will produce 20% to 30% greater results. In the case of B2B cold calling, that 1% will yield 75% to 80% more productivity. That is a surprisingly small amount of pain in exchange for a substantial level of gain.

Prospecting Numbers – The Stat's Tell the Story

Based upon national statistics, if you cold call 10 new businesses in person every day, you will present your product an average of 3 times. Of those 3 presentations, you will close 1. You will achieve a 10% closing average on cold calls, and a 30% closing average on presentations.

If you exclusively tele-market to generate business prospects, you will average about 1 presentation for every 50 calls attempted. Most of those calls will result in hang-ups and put-offs. Of those you are able to present, if you are good on the phone, you will sell maybe 30%. That is a 2% presentation rate on cold calls and a 0.3% closing rate on presentations.

These are abysmal numbers. You are 10 times more likely to succeed in person than on the phone.

Telephone cold calling appeals to many salespeople because the idea of in-person rejection is more terrifying than wasting time on the phone. Additionally, the trouble of driving to a business district and going door to door seems arduous in comparison to the ease of picking up a telephone.

I have always said:

IT IS EASIER TO HANG UP A PHONE THAN IT IS TO GET RID OF A BODY

As we discuss in **B2B Cold Calling**, if you show up in person, the business has to deal with you. If you call, they merely hang up a phone handset to get rid of you.

The in-person cold call sales numbers above are conservative. They are computed based upon your competitors door knocking too. I have news, they aren't door knocking. At best, they are cold calling on the phone. More likely, your competitors are relying on digital or media marketing or digital or media marketing with a telephone follow-up. Either way, the buyer is ready for them. Again, it is much easier to hang up a 10-ounce phone than it is to get rid of a visiting salesperson.

When you walk into a business, you are a viable presence. As far as they know, you may be a customer. As such, you will get a moment to sell. A phone hang-up will never give you that opportunity.

THE B2B IN-PERSON COLD CALL

1. **Walk into the office empty handed or with only a portfolio and a pen. -** A business card in hand is your ticket to ride – out of their office.
2. **Ask the gatekeeper a question about the company.** The first person you meet is the gatekeeper. He or she is a pro at filtering the customers from the salespeople. (Much of the filtering skill amongst gatekeepers has faded with the reduction in door to door sales these days.) **Do you provide this product?** (fill in with what you assume they sell or create as a business.) The answer will get the gatekeeper onto the *potential customer dialogue* rather than the *sales defense dialogue.*
3. **Acknowledge his or her reply with a confirming comment**: I didn't realize your company was as (large, diversified, successful, well-known) as you are. This compliment creates an obligation owed from the gatekeeper to return the warm regard. You will collect that debt as information.
4. **Who provides your product or service?** (who provides your telecom, who services your copiers, uniforms, pest control, etc?) Position the question so that your area of interest is general. You don't want to ask, *who sold you guys that Canon printer.* Your relationship with the gatekeeper is not mature enough to get specific information. Even if the competing vendor's name is

displayed, still ask the question. Don't say, "I know Acme Anvils provides your anvils." The purpose of the conversation is to get the prospect comfortable talking with you. By this time, you have revealed to the gatekeeper that you are a seller. Expect the gatekeeper to go on defense – that is his or her job.

5. **They are a great company and one of our biggest competitors. How long ago did you switch to them?** (Answer from the gatekeeper: *a few months, a year, etc.*) **That has been long enough for you to get to know them. Have they done everything you expected?** Don't ask how long their company has worked with them. The *switch to them* question style reminds the gatekeeper that they had someone else providing that service prior to the current vendor.
6. **Always compliment them on their choice**. Even if you know absolutely that the vendor is the smallest, newest, lowest-rated company with which you compete, commend them on making a good decision. Slinging mud at your competition will end with some of the splatter on you. The gatekeeper expects your reaction to the competitor to be negative, and it is a trap. Don't fall for it.
7. **Start your Pre-Presentation.** This is the elevator speech version of the presentation you will give to the decision maker.
8. **Close the sale. *Would you be willing to give us a try?*** Any closing question will do. It is possible that the gate keeper is the decision maker, but unlikely. The answer from the gatekeeper will be one of the following:
    - **a.** *We don't make that decision here. It is done at corporate.*
    - **b.** *I don't make that decision and he is out of the office or in a meeting right now.*
    - **c.** *We are happy with our current vendor.*

9. If the decision maker is in a corporate location, ask: **Who should I ask for when I reach out to them?** If the decision maker is local, ask: **Can John spare a quick moment for a question so I can prepare a quote?** If the person is not available or at the corporate office, get the contact information for the decision-maker. By mentioning that you want the info for a quote, you have removed the need for the gatekeeper to resist you further. The gatekeeper will believe that you are a proposer or estimator, harmless and benign. If the decision maker is local, the gatekeeper will check with him or her. If the gatekeeper says the decision maker works by appointment, ask: **Do you keep his/her calendar or does he/she? Set the appointment.**
10. If the answer is that they are happy with their current vendor, here is your response. **Of course, you are. You would probably be looking for my company if you weren't. I am only asking for the opportunity to compete for your business. Who makes that decision here?**

A Pause for Tender Feelings – It's going to be Okay

Reading this section, you may feel that the seller is pressuring the gatekeeper. Look beyond the person to person dynamic. Like your company, their business makes its living by selling its product or service. They need the product or service you offer whether they buy it from you or not.

The gatekeeper was hired to direct certain callers or visitors to an appropriate contact within the office. Your request is reasonable and acceptable. The gatekeeper's only issue with you is that you are an uninvited salesperson. Your company's product, service, reputation, or ability to provide a quality product is not at issue here.

If the company decides to buy from you, they will benefit from the decision. You are making it easy for them to achieve that benefit.

THE FIRST CONTACT WITH THE BUYER - TELEPHONE

If you are not cold calling your prospects, it is likely that you are generating your leads from a digital source or from advertising.

Sometimes prospective buyers call your office. Other times they email or fill out an information request online. When you answer the inbound call, or you call the prospect, you will begin **Setting the Table for the Sales Process** with your first impression.

In-home sales and commercial sales have many things in common. One of the most common is their habit of doing things in threes. They always get three bids.

Interior Designers provide three choices. Sears used to sell three levels of quality: Good, Better and Best. Consumers always get three bids.

Why do buyers believe that three bids will get them the best product or service at the most competitive price? The answer is as varied as it is irrelevant.

Requesting bids is a safety net. Requesting three bids is a defense mechanism meant to create an assurance of the most competitive price through disparate sources.

Essentially, the buyer is afraid of being ripped off or taken advantage of and doesn't know who to trust. In most cases you, the seller, are the marketing research portion of their buying decision. When they request a bid, their expectation of you is that of a resource by which they can compare the other two. Remember, a proposal has no sales ability.

MOST BUYERS MAKE THE BUYING DECISION ONLY AFTER THEY HAVE SATISFIED THEIR FEARS OF DANGER FROM THE SELLER.

It is the professional seller's job to allay that fear during his or her time in front of the buyer.

The Warm Lead

The difference between a *Cold Call* and a *Warm Lead* is who makes first contact. If the seller approaches the buyer first, it is generally a **Cold Call**. If the buyer reaches out to the seller, it is a **Warm Lead**.

To demonstrate the steps of the first telephone call for a **Warm Lead**, let's use the home improvement industry for our example. The product is technical, and the sales process is advanced. Your product or service may not require the level of detail as we will discuss in the home improvement example, but it is helpful to know more than you use, than to know less than you need.

As with most products or services, remodeling customers generally buy things with which they are familiar. Although not at a technical level, the prospect will know what he or she needs in general terms. Whether the seller has contracted a remodeler before, or only watched HGTV, he or she has a good idea what to expect in the purchase and delivery of the product. In addition to the desire for the successful production of their project, the buyer wants to hire a reputable firm with references, great reviews, and an established track record.

Using *Angie's List, Home Advisor, Thumbtack, Houz,* or any other subscription search engine, the buyer requests bids from suggested contractors who match their criteria. In most cases, the buyer will contact more than three contractors knowing that only three will be selected to bid.

Keep in mind that when the buyer takes your call, you are only one seller of many who will speak to the buyer. How do you set yourself apart from everyone else?

I have good news for you. From my years in remodeling sales, I learned firsthand that your competition is made primarily of former construction company owners and artisans. They are bidders and estimators with truly little sales experience.

Professional Selling has never been practiced on a job site or in a plan room. These experienced technical experts never learned to sell at a professional level.

WHERE THE TECHNICAL EXPERT WILL FOCUS ON THE TECHNICAL DETAILS OF THE PRODUCT OR SERVICE, THE PROFESSIONAL SELLER WILL FOCUS ON THE NEEDS OF THE BUYER.

When you receive the phone call, or you call the buyer, you want to **Set the Table for the Sales Process**. Foremost in your mind is that you are not an estimator, nor are you a bidder. You are a service provider whose features include a secure buying environment for the customer, and a fair price.

That first contact is the seller's first chance to make one of many sales to the buyer. You must sell an appointment. You must also sell a process. Eliminate the competition by showing sincere interest and genuine insight.

Here is how you do it:

Set the Appointment

Seller: *Hello, Jack. This is Craig with Acme Remodeling. Thanks for taking my call. Do you have a moment to chat?*

Buyer: *Hello, Craig. I do have time.*

Seller: *I understand that you are taking bids for your bathroom remodel and you want us to compete for your business, is that right?*

Buyer: *Yes, we are. The bathroom is a hall bath with a tub. We want to convert the tub to a shower, a new vanity, and we want new tile.*

Seller: *It sounds like you have done your research. Have you set a date when you want the project completed?*

Buyer: *We are in no hurry. We are getting prices right now.*

Seller: *A wise plan. How many bids do you plan to get?*

Buyer: *We are taking three bids.*

Seller: *Good idea. Am I the first or the last on your list?*

Buyer: *We just started. You are the second so far.*

Seller: *Excellent. When do you plan to have your bidding completed?*

Buyer: *We want to have all our bids completed by the end of the month.*

Seller: *You mentioned we. Is there another person involved in the decision making for the project?*

Buyer: *My wife and I own the home.*

Seller: *What is her name?*

Buyer: *Her name is Jill.*

Seller: *It sounds like we had better get together soon. Do you and Jill have a prescribed budget for your project?*

Buyer: *We really have no idea what a bathroom remodel costs.*

Seller: *Many of our customers started that way. A bathroom renovation is pretty technical, with all the licensed trades and differences in finishes selections. Do you anticipate that most of your bids will be in the thousands or tens of thousands range?*

Buyer: *Probably tens of thousands. Hopefully no more than $20,000.00.*

Seller: *Your budget is a bit low, but I think we can get close to that. At $20,000.00 am I still in range to earn your business?*

Buyer: *I think so.*

Seller: *Are you asking your bidders to provide a credit option or are you funded already?*

Buyer: *We have the money in savings.*

Seller: *Great. Being that you want your bids completed by the end of the month, can the three of us meet this week, say Tuesday at 3pm or what about Thursday morning before noon?*

Buyer: *Tuesday at 3 works for both of us.*

Seller: *Perfect. I will see you both at 3pm on Tuesday. Thank you.*

Components of the Appointment Call

1. **Greeting** - Be sure to thank them for contacting you. Confirm they are considering buying from you and you expect them to do business with you.
2. **Urgency** – Establishing a deadline will play a role in follow-ups.
3. **Competition** - Know how many, and with whom, you are competing. Ask for a name. If they share the competitor's information, compliment them on their choices of bidders. When the buyer reveals the competition, it is easier to sell against them.
4. **Where are you in the Process** – Find out if you are the first to bid. Learn how long they plan to take bids. This will tell you about their urgency to buy. If they have no urgency, ask them why they are starting the process now, being that

pricing may change drastically if they wait to move on the bid.

5. **Identify the Decision-Makers** – Never *One-Leg a pitch.* Involve all decision makers in the process. If your sales process is an initial fact gathering appointment, you may opt to one-leg it. Understand that if you do, you will have to review everything discussed and agreed upon during the fact-finding appointment when you sit for the Proposal Appointment. It is best to have all decision-makers present each time. A one-leg guarantees the objection *I need to think about it.*
6. **Budget** – Price condition the buyer. Many times, the buyer has no idea what your product or service costs, or they feel your price may be lower than they expect, and they don't want you to take advantage of a high budget number. More commonly, you learn their budget number to prequalify them. Are they a serious buyer? Is your understanding of what they want accurate? Are they funded? Finally, knowing their budget positions you to ask for the business in a convincing way.
7. **Appointment** – Set the appointment with all decision makers using the *Alternate Choice Question Form. Tuesday at 3pm or what about Thursday morning before noon?*
8. **Thank them for the Appointment** – Make your last impression a good one.

[4]

Chapter 4 – Warm-up Q&A

Arrival To The First Appointment

What you do at this point in the sales process will determine to a large degree whether you earn the sale or not. This is the first date in an important relationship of which you want to be a part. Make no mistake, you are on trial for your sales life. The buyer knows only that you are one of three bidders for a project about which he or she knows little.

In our bathroom renovation example, the buyer may have already met with one if not both or your competitors. In other industries the buyer may have purchased the product or service before.

Your competitor may have provided the buyer his or her only experience with the process. It is possible that the buyer has never met with a professional seller before, and he or she will attempt to guide the interview based upon how your competitor handled the previous appointment. Be kind. Likely, the buyer is well-intentioned and wants to make the appointment quick and efficient.

You arrive at the door early or on time, you decide which works best for you. Never be late. To the buyer, this is a job interview and he or she is evaluating everything you say and do.

Jack opens the door and lets you in. Jill waits further away inside. You enter, handing Jack your business card, greeting Jill as you do.

"Let me show you the bathroom", Jack says and turns to lead you to the work location.

The buyers' understanding of how the appointment will go is based upon practicality and experiences with previous sellers. It is rare that a home improvement salesperson will not go immediately to the bathroom to measure and take notes.

You, however, will not do that. Your job is to **Set the Table for the Sales Process**. The product or service is a given. You will demonstrate your value as a sales professional. Your efforts will focus upon earning the credibility and trust you will need to disengage their **Buyer Defense Mechanism** and ultimately close the sale.

WARMUP Q&A

The pleasant chit chat is over. The pressure is on the seller to create an environment where the project, product or service, and the seller's credibility must be established as a priority in the buyer's decision-making process.

Maybe the buyer has seen your type of product on TV. Maybe your competition has already presented their products or services. One way or another the buyer has preconceived notions about what you will say and how you will position yourself as the best choice.

When I say, "The pleasant chit chat is over," you may think, "When did the pleasant chit chat begin?"

Your time with the buyer is valuable to you and the buyer. Make no mistake, when you arrived, you punched a time clock. You have only a limited amount of time to make your points and leave. The buyer is not consciously aware of a time limit, nor is the buyer holding a stopwatch, but his or her natural sense of time passing will determine when you have worn out your welcome.

The seller must approach the **Warmup Q&A** in a friendly, but businesslike fashion. You are not there to make friends, although you do want the buyer to like you. People buy from people they like. If the buyer doesn't like you or is ambivalent towards you, he or she will not buy from you.

Being friendly without being too familiar is critical at this point. Are you liked by everyone who has ever met you? No. How can you ensure that natural dynamic doesn't affect the relationship between you and your buyer? You can't completely. However, through subject-based, insightful questions, delivered with genuine interest and concern, you will place the odds on your side.

The more personal insight they gain about you, the greater the odds that the buyer will find something about you to which he or she objects. This is a professional relationship. Treat is as such.

Fish on The Wall

Most amateur salespeople open a sales visit with a *Fish on the Wall* conversation. Mistakenly, the seller believes that he or she will develop rapport with the buyer by showing interest in them personally.

In a sales relationship, the seller has been invited to the buyer's office or home. Often the seller looks around the room and sees a fish on the wall, golf clubs, family photos, cat toys, etc. and starts a conversation about the personal items in the room. In the sales business we call this a distraction. When a seller engages in this type of counterproductive chit chat, he or she puts the entire sales process at risk.

THESE ARE THE LIKELY RESULTS OF FISH ON THE WALL CONVERSATIONS:

1. THE BUYER WILL POLITELY SHARE THE PERSONAL INFORMATION WITH YOU - A COMPLETE STRANGER - BUT SILENTLY RESENT THE INTRUSION.
2. THE BUYER HAS ALLOTTED A SPECIFIC TIME OUT OF HIS OR HER DAY FOR THE INTERVIEW AND WILL FEEL THE TIME IS WASTED ON NON-PRODUCT OR SERVICE CHIT CHAT.
3. AS THE BUYER GETS TO KNOW THE SELLER, THEY DECIDE THEY DON'T LIKE THEM EITHER PERSONALLY OR PHILOSOPHICALLY.
4. THE SELLER MAY APPEAR TO BE AN AMATEUR, INEPT, AND UNENGAGED IN THE URGENCY OF THE SALES PROPOSITION.
5. THE BUYER FINDS A NEW FRIEND AND THE SELLER IS INVITED OVER FOR DINNER AND DOUBLE DATES WITH THE BUYER AND SPOUSE.

None of these serves the sales process. As a professional seller, you must define the relationship as a professional one, seasoned with genuine interest in their needs and delivered with warm regard. You must be likeable, but not overly friendly; interested, but not creepy.

Years ago, I visited a couple who were in the market for a home renovation. My sales manager joined me on the appointment. He was the same fellow I told you about who hired only project managers on his sales team. I followed the steps in the Warmup Q&A. We came to the project inspection phase and I began measuring.

The manager chatted with the buyer while I measured. As we moved through the home, we passed the husband's office. The sales manager looked inside and spotted a collection of professional sports memorabilia. The sales manager had played pro sports and he moved the conversation onto the collection.

I could not catch my sales manager's eye, nor did he allow my control phrases to derail his zeal as he talked about the buyer's collection.

I measured the project alone.

In your sales process, if you are in an industry where you are bringing a product or service into a buyer's home or business, the inspection phase is critical in helping the buyer to establish ownership of your product or service. As you inspect or measure, you must ask questions to which the answers develop a sense of ownership between the buyer and your product or service.

Because he took the owners away from the project area to pursue a point of outside interest, the sales manager relegated my efforts to that of an order taker or estimator.

An interesting side note on these buyers: the couple had called us to take over a project that had been abandoned by another contractor. They were in a lawsuit with the previous remodeler and had informed us that they were suspicious of all remodelers. Every moment of the sales interview was critical for rebuilding their trust in the industry by demonstrating our interest in their project and genuine concern for their needs.

I don't believe the buyers' needs were addressed by spending fifteen minutes admiring their sports collection. We did not get the sale. They went with another builder.

The sales manager violated almost every rule of the sales process. I can't guarantee that we would have gotten the sale otherwise, but the point of the sales process is to increase the chances that the buyer will buy from you.

Qualifying Questions

From the moment you meet with the buyer, you must demonstrate sincere interest and concern as it applies to the sales offer.

Without bringing flowers and a sweet card, how do you do that?

In the sales business it is rare for the buyer to reveal everything he or she thinks, wants, or fears in a purchasing situation. The seller is a stranger at this point. The questions the seller ask reveal much of this information. The questions also indicate to the buyer that the seller is interested in his or her needs.

The mutual exchange of information, the buyer's answers to questions, and the seller's connecting the product or service, and the features and benefits to those needs, creates a relationship between buyer and seller.

Qualifying Questions are designed to identify what the buyer sees as the important aspects of the product or service. These are *Hot Button* items for the buyer. Qualifying Questions serve to help the seller tie those Hot Buttons to the particulars of the offer. Most importantly,

QUALIFYING QUESTIONS HELP TO CREATE A DYNAMIC AND GENUINE SALES RELATIONSHIP BETWEEN THE BUYER AND THE SELLER.

The seller's credibility is founded in that relationship. Without the relationship, the seller will not close the sale.

Types of Qualifying Questions

The most common definition for a qualifying question is a question to which the answer confirms that the buyer needs or wants what the product or service offers.

I believe that the true definition of a Qualifying Question is a question to which the answer confirms that the prospect is buying the seller, and what he or she is doing. When the question is asked during an engaging conversation rather than posed as an

itemized question in an interview, it serves to create interest from the buyer and expresses interest by the seller.

Unlike closing questions that confirm the prospect is buying, Qualifying Questions determine which way the prospect will buy.

- **IS THE PRODUCT APPROPRIATE FOR THE BUYER?**
- **IS THE BUYER APPROPRIATE FOR THE COMPANY?**
- **WHO IS THE COMPETITION?**
- **WHY DID THE BUYER AGREE TO MEET WITH THE SELLER?**
- **IS THE BUYER A CASH BUYER?**
- **WHO ELSE IS INVOLVED WITH THE BUYER IN THE DECISION MAKING?**
- **IS THE BUYER PREPARED TO MOVE ON THE OFFER ONCE IT IS PRESENTED?**
- **WHAT ARE THE OBSTACLES TO OVERCOME IN ORDER TO DO BUSINESS?**
- **WHAT IS IT ABOUT THE PRODUCT THAT CAN BE MADE A PERSONAL BENEFIT FOR THE BUYER?**

Qualifying Questions should always be interrogative, beginning with the words: *Where, When, What, How, Which, and Why.* They must never be answered with a yes or no.

The purpose is to get the buyer to talk about himself or herself as it relates to the product or service. Only through the buyer's participation in the conversation can the seller create the bond he or she will need to develop the sales relationship, and the credibility required to apply the sales tools we cover in this book.

People love to talk about themselves. If you allow the buyer to enjoy the conversation and bask in the light of personal recognition, the buyer will warm to you. Many sellers present their product or service in a monologue of information. Buyers quickly lose interest in seminar presentations.

Include the buyer in your presentation by asking Qualifying Questions throughout your sales presentation.

Introduce Pain into the Process

This next concept may seem counter-intuitive if you don't understand the necessity for a measure of discomfort in the sales process. Most salespeople avoid causing the buyer pain. As a result, the salesperson receives pain of his or her own.

How do you make a sweet dessert sweeter? You add a pinch of salt to the mix. A plastic surgeon told me once that the features we find most attractive in others are considered flaws in the medical realm. In art, the quality of a painter's work is measured by the flaws that define the painter's stroke as genius. You have heard the saying "It's too good to be true."

All of these demonstrate our expectation of pain, discomfort, trouble, or complications in all things.

What a Seller Says, the Buyer Tends to Doubt

It is human nature. That little bit of larceny that resides within us all causes us to distrust others. We secretly believe that others will act in a self-serving way rather than magnanimously.

If the seller paints a picture of perfection and ease, the buyer will necessarily look for the *other shoe to drop* scenario.

Honesty is rarely painless. We learned this when we were told that Santa Claus and the Easter Bunny are not real.

The customer has taken great pains to protect himself from the inevitable pain he is certain will occur as he is separated from his money, to own your product or service. The buyer carefully checked your company's reviews, references, and background. He knows the stories of sellers taking advantage of buyers. He took three bids just to make sure you were being truthful with your pricing. The buyer knows there are inherent dangers in doing business, particularly with a salesperson.

If you try to sell him a Utopian sales fantasy, he will grow suspicious. Your credibility will suffer a grave hit.

The reason you want to introduce pain into the sale is to earn credibility. In the insurance business it is called

"BACK THE HEARSE UP TO THE DOOR AND LET THEM SMELL THE FLOWERS."

Whenever you present your product or service to a buyer, tell stories of how things went wrong when past buyers purchased from someone else.

This may blow your mind. Warn the buyer of inherent dangers or discomfort if he or she buys from you. I don't recommend you share experiences from dissatisfied former customers. Don't tell the buyer you have a couple of bad reviews. You want to be general in your warnings. Assign the pain to the industry. The remodeling business is one of the most insidious industries there is. Warn the buyer of the inherent hazards of the industry.

If you are selling cars and the buyer wants a black one, let him know that the car is beautiful, but the sun really heats up the interior of a black car. Doing this will give his anticipated pain a place to go.

In the remodeling industry, it is always wise to get an idea what the buyer believes the price will be for the project. The seller should always ask the buyer's budget number.

The budget question is one of the best opportunities to apply pain to the process. Most often, the buyer will give the seller a low, or sometimes, an unrealistic budget number. The seller will inform the buyer that the anticipated budget is a bit low for the complexity of the project.

When I sold in the remodeling industry and I was given a low budget number, many times I handled it like this:

> ***Buyer:*** *My budget is $ 20,000.00*
>
> ***Seller:*** *That is a bit low for the scope of work you are planning. Where did you get that number?*
>
> ***Buyer:*** *I have gotten bids at that price from your competition.*
>
> ***Seller:*** *Many of my customers experienced this same phenomenon. The construction business is the easiest industry for anyone to enter. Someone might have been working for Microsoft last week and got laid off. This week they are in the construction business. You will typically get three levels of bidders. The low prices generally indicate desperation to make a sale. Why would a legitimate remodeling firm be desperate in a booming economy? The high bidders are generally afraid of the job because they don't know much about it. A high price covers them in case they make a big mistake. The ones in the middle are generally playing from the playbook of experience and competition. We tend to be in the middle. Under what circumstance would you seriously consider elevating your budget?*

The seller has applied pain derived from his or her insight in the industry. Uncomfortable as it is for the buyer, the seller's insight will contribute to the seller's credibility.

Whenever you distribute pain, always follow it with a first aid treatment. In the case of the black car, add to your warning,

> *"All of my customers who purchased a black car agree that the beauty, and how the car makes them feel when they drive it, far outweigh the possibility of overheating the interior. Don't you agree?"*

We will cover this in the *Question Forms* section, but that last question is a *Tie Down Question*.

As a seller, never make a statement in selling unless you attach a question at the end. Tie it down.

Asking for a Budget Number

Since we are on the subject, let's talk about how to ask for a buyer's budget number. If you struggle with asking for a budget, don't despair.

For most of us, asking a customer what they are willing to pay for a product or service is counterintuitive. Our Buyer Defense Mechanism sounds a klaxon bell in our heads, and we reject the notion.

If you are a seller who assembles pricing then proposes the number, you have the advantage over the retailer or the seller whose price is advertised. You also have a great disadvantage.

In the remodeling industry, pricing can vary wildly. Builders and remodelers price projects as they see fit. Although materials and labor are priced similarly, builders' calculation strategies differ greatly. Some estimate costs based upon square footage, product costs and hard bids. Others base pricing upon experience and high round numbers they anticipate for trades and materials.

The buyer's budget may have come from a competitor's bid, friends' experiences, an HGTV remodeling show, or a practical guess. It is important that the seller learns what the buyer believes he or she should pay for the product or service the seller is bidding.

If the seller never learns this information and produces a proposal, the *I Need to Think About It* objection is sure to arise. The seller will never learn that the buyer has only $20,000.00 for the project and has no idea what the cost could be.

Asking for the budget number also opens the conversation to include helping the buyer secure financing; reveal additional work; and learning how serious the buyer is about the purchase.

The buyer will resist giving the budget for the same reason you find the question counterintuitive.

Here is how you handle it:

Seller: *Do you mind if I ask you an important question?*

Buyer: *No, we don't mind.*

Seller: *If I were selling used cars, siding and storm windows, or insurance, you should never answer this question. However, as your remodeling expert, I need to ask you, what is your anticipated budget for this project?*

Buyer: *We don't know. That is why we are taking bids.*

Seller: *I understand. Most of my customers invited me to their homes with a preset budget, either because the bank offered a set amount, or they had saved a set amount for the project. Do you have a hard cost over which you can't go?*

Buyer: *We hope the project won't be more than $20,000.00.*

If the budget is workable:

Seller: *That is a realistic budget. I will make it my goal to keep the scope of the project limited to one that will fall beneath that number.*

If the budget is low:

Seller: *That is not a bad start. Where did you get that number for a project of this size and technical requirements? Did a builder offer that price or has someone told you that is what it should cost?*

Buyer: *It is all we have to invest in the project right now.*

Seller: *I understand. I live by the same rules in my life. Under what circumstance would you seriously consider elevating your budget?*

Buyer: *How much do you think it will be?*

Seller: *You mentioned to me that you are selecting your bidders carefully, so may I assume that the other remodelers are of the same caliber as my company?*

Buyer: *Yes.*

Seller: *That is a wise decision. Amongst reputable companies, a project of this type will be around $25,000.00. Is that something you can work with?*

This technique will reveal the budget and the reasons and circumstances that caused the buyer to arrive at that number. It also creates an opportunity for the seller to demonstrate his or her value in the decision process. Most importantly, the seller has offered a trial close and the buyer has made a commitment to the seller.

The fear of asking for the budget is widespread with salespeople. The Buyer Defense Mechanism in us all rebels against it. If you conquer your fears and open the door to the issue, the buyer will feel closer to you, because he or she has shared a personal story with you. One of the buyer's concerns is now a shared concern. The professional seller will acknowledge the issue and offer a solution. The solution may be to help them end their buying process because they are not prepared for the price tag. Either way, the seller has helped the buyer in a measurable way.

Review - Structure of the First Appointment

1. **Show up on time or early** – Your dependability, and that of your company is represented by how you present yourself to the buyer. **Thank you for inviting me.**
2. **Would you mind if we take a moment to get acquainted?** – Meet with the buyer at the table or in the living room. If a business, meet in the buyer's office or a conference room.
3. **Warm-Up Q&A: Ask Qualifying Questions** – Clarify what the buyer needs and expects from you. Learn his or her concerns and fears as they pertain to the product or service. **Introduce a measure of pain into the conversation**. Much of the Warm-up Q&A will be a review from your appointment call. It is good to repeat the questions. The repeated information with the buyer shares the answers with the other decision makers, refreshes the answer, and is more effective on site.
   a. **How long have you owned the home?** The answer helps you know the reasons for the remodel and if they have equity in their home or need financing.
   b. **Is this the only project you are planning?** There may be additional business there.
   c. **Have you renovated before? How did that go?** You can learn more about their fears and why they bought before.
   d. **How long do you plan to own your home?** Are they renovating to sell or for their future? Don't ask the buyer how long they have lived in the home. The ownership context keeps the business aspect of the visit front and center.
   e. **Have the other bidders visited yet? Were they on time? How did they do? What do you recommend I do so that we optimize our time together?** Learn where you are in their buying process. Place importance on the time they are investing in the process.

f. **Has anything changed since we spoke on the phone?** If your competitors have visited, the buyer will have learned new information. The scope of work may have changed.
g. **How did you find us?** This is optional. You will probably know where you got the lead.

Your Warm-up Q&A should be structured as an interesting conversation. You must acknowledge each answer and, if appropriate, connect the answer with an aspect of your product or service. Do not interrogate the buyer.

4. **Company / Product Presentation** - If the product presentation depends upon a site survey or facility inspection, present only your company and the general features and benefits of your product or service. In the case of our bathroom project, present your company's renovation services as you measure and inspect the project site.
5. **Close the Sale** - Every customer appointment ends with a sale being made. This is your second close in the process. In part, this gets the buyer used to buying from you, making the final decision a bit easier.
   a. **Review the product or service options they have agreed to purchase.** Word your review as if you have already been awarded the sale. "So, we are going to remove the tub and move the existing drain to the center, is that correct?"
   b. **Set the parameters of their commitment to you in exchange for the next appointment and the work you are going to have to perform for them.** *It will take me a few days to put your proposal together. I need to consult with my trades, price out the materials, and build a comprehensive proposal. You mentioned that you wanted to have the project completed by Thanksgiving, didn't you?*

In order to do that we will need to get started within the next two weeks. Are you prepared to make a decision on your bids that quickly?

c. **Close** – Set the proposal appointment. Ask for the buyer's commitment to make a decision when you return. *You told me that you have placed a deadline of the end of the month for your bids and you have a $25,000.00 budget. You want to hire the most reputable and knowledgeable contractor, and you told me that you want to complete the project by Thanksgiving. If you feel that I have fulfilled all these requirements, is there any reason we can't set a start date when I return with the completed proposal?*

d. **Reduce pressure if they will not commit** – You will have an opportunity to close the sale during the Proposal Appointment. Whether they commit or not, they now know that you are expecting to earn their business at your next appointment. If you have followed the process, most buyers will commit to you to make a decision at the Proposal Appointment.

A Pause for Tender Feelings – It's going to be Okay

Why would the buyer commit to you? If you were the buyer, you would never agree to make a decision, would you? You don't buy that way, and you don't like high pressure salespeople who sell that way!

Hold on, my tender-hearted friend. You are reacting to the magic because you have seen behind the curtain. You know what we are trying to achieve. You naturally root for the buyer. This is your Buyer Defense Mechanism engaging.

Didn't the buyer invite you to come by and offer your product or service? You didn't force the buyer to look for your product or service. The buyer is wanting to purchase your product or service. The buyer has already gone through an arduous research and fact-finding mission to buy from you. Your presentation has allayed many fears he or she may have preconceived or known in fact. The buyer likes you and believes in you.

Your work there has helped the buyer to prioritize his or her buying decision. Asking him or her to take that additional step with you is serving the relationship with you as a partner in the project, product, or service. Remember, the buyer doesn't know who to trust. You are helping him or her to decide.

Again, you will notice a developing theme in this book. The odds are extremely good that your competitors are not professional sellers. Based upon national statistics, they are almost guaranteed to be unskilled in sales. They will not ask the questions you ask; they will go directly to the project site; they will apply no pain and assure the buyer everything is going to be perfect; they will probably email the proposal; and they will not ask for the business.

For the buyer, the most natural and reasonable conclusion to the sales process is to buy. If you ask for the business, your odds of getting it are exponentially greater than if you fire off a proposal.

If you do email a proposal, you better hope you are the lowest bidder, or more sadly, that one of your competitors isn't a pro and asks for the sale.

[5]

CHAPTER 5 – THE PROPOSAL PRESENTATION

THE PROPOSAL PRESENTATION APPOINTMENT

Today is the day of the show. You have **Set the Table for the Sales Process**. Part of that preparation included establishing your importance in the buying process. You have also earned credibility with the buyer as an expert. They trust you to help them make the best buying decision.

You must affect the same manner and sales personality you did on the 1st appointment. Remember, the customer buys you and what you are doing. You give them the product for free. If you change what you are doing, or how you are perceived, the buyer will grow uncomfortable.

Join the buyer at the table or wherever you met previously for the **Warmup Q&A**. All parties must be present throughout the proposal presentation. A one Leg Pitch will end in the deadly **I Need to Think About It** objection.

Review the questions and answers you asked at the first appointment. This time, you include their answers from before, tying the answer down with a question or comment. Each time ask their agreement that you are accurate in your understanding. After they acknowledge that your understanding of their needs is identical to their understanding, ask a question.

Since we last met, has anything changed?

It is likely that the buyer has met with your competitors. It is typical that the other bidders introduced new ideas, additional products, or services, and created new concerns.

When the buyer indicates he or she has more questions or concerns, or he or she has learned more about the process or product, ask a question.

Have you met with the other companies since we last met?

You must learn what the buyer liked and disliked about the other offers. This is important for several reasons.

1. If the scope of work has changed, or the product offering has changed, you need to know if your proposal is still valid and accurate.
2. The buyer will reveal his or her impressions of the competitors and whether he or she liked them or not.
3. You will learn if you are still important to them in the sales process.
4. Finally, the information you receive will help you to eliminate the competition as your presentation proceeds.

Find out as much as you can about the competition. Always speak highly of the competition. Compliment the buyer for assembling reputable bidders for his or her buying decision.

- Inquire whether the buyer has received pricing from the competition.
- If yes, did their pricing come close to the buyer's budget?
- If the competition has not presented a price, ask when they promised to return with a price.
- Ask the buyer how your expertise compares to the competition. If the buyer compliments you, thank the

buyer for his or her support and enter the competition elimination phase.

Eliminate the Competition

Although you have Set the Table for the Sales Process, earned Credibility, and created a relationship with the buyer, he or she will remain committed to getting other bids. This was the initial plan, and you have not, and should not, try to alter it. The buyer plans to eliminate the competition one way or the other as a part of the bidding process.

THERE CAN BE ONLY ONE!

Your efforts to eliminate the competition during your sales presentation ultimately serve the buyer's expectations.

Never sling mud at the competition. The buyer expects this, and it is a trap he or she has set to help eliminate bidders. Remember:

WHAT THE SELLER SAYS, THE BUYER TENDS TO DOUBT

Remember this dynamic throughout your Sales Process.

Continuing our role play with the remodeling buyer, here is the way you do it:

Seller: *Jack and Jill, it sounds like things are going smoothly in the bidding phase of your project. Are you still committed to having your buying decision made by the end of the month?*

Buyer: *We want to stick with our original time schedule, but we haven't received all the estimates.*

Seller: *I understand how you feel. What are you going to do if these companies don't meet your deadline?*

Buyer: *I guess we wait.*

Seller: *Let me ask you a different question. What would you say to a company who promised you that they would start your job on a specified day and failed to meet that obligation? (Don't pause) What if a company promised to complete your project on a specified day and failed to meet it?(don't pause) Jack and Jill, what if they did both and didn't call you in advance to communicate that they would not meet their obligations promised you?*

Buyer: *I would not be happy.*

Seller: *Of course, you wouldn't. Would you recommend a company who fails to meet deadlines, without a call, to your family or friends?*

Buyer: *No, I wouldn't, but this isn't the same thing.*

Seller: *Isn't it? When we met, you told me that you wanted to hire the best company for your project. You shared with me that your number one concern was reliability and communication. Did you share these requirements with the other companies?*

Buyer: *Yes, we did.*

Seller: *I thought so. I took your requirements seriously. My staff and I invested many late hours on the research, pricing, and production of a final proposal in order to be here on time as I promised we would. Don't you agree that if a company can't do something simple like producing a proposal on time, they might have a difficult time starting and completing something as technically difficult as your project?*

Buyer: *Maybe.*

Seller: *I doubt you would tolerate it if I did it, would you?*

Buyer: *Probably not.*

Seller: *When Acme Remodelers was founded 30 years ago, the owners pledged that each time a customer stepped into our showroom, or we visited a customer in their home, we would do as much as is possible to satisfy the customer and meet their expectations. Why would you settle for less?*

Buyer: *We wouldn't.*

Seller: *I agree with you. May I show you what I came up with?*

If your product is not dependent upon proposals, or the other bidders have met their obligations, you must still eliminate the competition.

Here is how you do it:

Seller: *Jack and Jill, it sounds like things are going smoothly in the bidding phase of your project. Are you still committed to having your buying decision made by the end of the month?*

Buyer: *Yes, we are. You are the final bidder.*

Seller: *Congratulations on meeting your deadline. Based upon the bids you have received; are you close to a decision?*

Buyer: *We want to see what you offer before we decide.*

Seller: *I appreciate that. Let me ask you a question. If all the prices were identical, how would you make your decision?*

Buyer: *I guess we would go with the best company.*

Seller: *How would you determine that?*

Buyer: *We would check out their reviews, maybe get references or customer referrals.*

Seller: *You have probably already researched this, haven't you?*

Buyer: *Of course. I mean, we have done a lot of looking at them.*

Seller: *Great. Does any company stand out presently? How am I doing so far?*

Buyer: *We like you. You are one of the finalists, but the price will have a big impact on our decision.*

Seller: *I am glad to hear that. When Acme Remodelers was founded 30 years ago, the owners pledged that each time a customer stepped into our showroom, or we visited a customer in their home, we would do as much as is possible to satisfy the customer and meet their expectations. Why would you settle for less?*

Buyer: *We wouldn't.*

Seller: *I agree with you. May I show you what I came up with?*

You have planted a seed at this point. During your presentation you will include a commitment to your company as part of your sales process.

Eliminating the competition is a gradual process. This is the first step of several you will employ to elevate your company. In the least, you want to create doubt in the buyer's perception of the competition. If, as in the Jack and Jill roleplay, you have solid evidence of a negative experience with the competition, ask for agreement that they wouldn't tolerate it from you and should not tolerate it from anyone who wants to earn their business.

Present the Proposal

I believe you should never give the buyer a copy of the proposal and/or technical drawing unless they buy from you. It is easier to hand over a copy and review the details with the buyer, but that is the path of least resistance. Your competitors are certain to be following the path of least resistance. You should not.

Consider your effort and expertise in the creation of your sales presentation. If you were to divide your work hours and the tasks you perform daily into the total of your work week, where would you guess you spend the most of your time? More precisely, how much of your time is spent presenting your product or service to a buyer?

Prospecting and lead generation may be the largest part of the work day for the hard-working door to door or cold call seller. If your leads are generated via lead sources or search engines, likely you spend the most of your time on proposal creation. You may spend as little as 10% of your total workday on presenting to the buyer.

WHY WOULD YOU GIVE AWAY 90% OF YOUR WORK AT NO CHARGE?

Is your time worth nothing? If you present your efforts that way to the buyer, it will appear that your time has little or no value. Why would anyone value your work if you don't?

One company I worked with included a free design drawing with every remodeling proposal we generated. Most of the sellers gave copies of both to the buyer. It was a common thing to see our design built by another builder. More often, the free drawing elicited early objections from the buyer.

If the buyer dislikes the design, the drawing will necessarily need to be altered or updated before business can be negotiated. The result is a longer sales cycle, unnecessary red flags for the buyer, and more free work for the seller.

B2B and non-remodeling companies know the dangers of giving away proprietary information. That is why most sellers carry a presentation manual or a tablet with a sales presentation saved to it.

The proposal is proprietary information. The work you put into the proposal has value. Never give away your effort and your skill set.

This is how you handle it:

> ***Buyer:*** *Can I get a copy of the proposal, so we can look over the details?*
>
> ***Seller:*** *I apologize. Our proposals are proprietary. The pricing and terms are yours to note, but we cannot leave company property behind.*
>
> ***Buyer:*** *You said the proposal was free.*
>
> ***Seller:*** *Oh, I understand the confusion. I mentioned that the consultation is free. The proposal and the drawing are company property. We will cover the details of the proposed work carefully today, and I will share the pricing and terms with you. Does that make sense?*

This may seem a bit brash, but you have just added value to the proposal and the work you invested in it. You have also introduced a measure of pain to the buyer. As we agreed earlier, a relationship must involve a little discomfort to be real. Your credibility is strengthened when you tell the buyer no and can justify it.

The buyer(s) should be beside you at the table so you can show them the proposal and point out areas of importance. Another benefit of having the only copy is that the buyer doesn't become impatient and hurry to the pricing page before you have had a chance to fully cover the offer.

Stay in control of the presentation. You know the process, the buyer does not. You invested a significant amount of time and effort for their benefit. You may or may not sell them. You have earned the right to ask for their time in return.

ITEMIZED PROPOSALS

It is possible that the buyer requested an itemized proposal from you at the 1st appointment. Many companies provide itemized pricing on their proposals. I have worked for a few that did. I have sold successfully both ways.

The inherent problem with itemized proposals is that you must price each component as if it were a stand-alone product or service, resulting in a higher total price.

For instance, if a builder priced a paint job where he proposed to paint ten doors for $1,000.00. The customer could easily opt to paint eight of the more easily painted doors himself and leave the two doors requiring the builder's specialized tools and expertise for the builder to paint. The buyer would expect those two doors to be painted for $200.00. That is hardly worth the trip for the builder. The job had been priced as a total package. The multiple door scope of work was priced where each door absorbed a portion of the typical and customary costs of doing business. The stand-alone price for each door would most likely be $200.00 each if they were priced separately.

In the case of itemizing, a proposal with multiple products or services would require a full markup on each component of the offer in case the buyer decides to decrease the quantity of purchased items.

If a buyer requests an itemized proposal, this is how you handle it: (Again we are following our remodeling role play.)

Buyer: *We are going to need an itemized proposal from you, with as much detail as you can include.*

Seller: *I understand, Jack. Why do you feel it would be to your advantage to have an itemized proposal?*

Buyer: *We have a limited budget and may want to cut back on some of the costs to keep the proposal under that number.*

Seller: *That makes sense to me. Didn't we agree that your budget was $25,000.00?*

Buyer: *Yes, but I want to pay the least I can for this project.*

Seller: *I understand how you feel. Most of my customers place a value on getting the most competitive price. Just to clarify my thinking, what do you think is the best price for this product?*

Buyer: *I'm not sure.*

Seller: *I wasn't either until I spent several hours putting together this proposal. In order to achieve the most competitive pricing, I had to work the numbers thoroughly. There are only a few places where a company can cut corners to lower the price. You see, Mr. Customer, an 8' wall stud is $2.15 in the Dominion* ***(nicest neighborhood in the area)*** *just like it is here. Our cost of doing business is a constant thing, so we can't lower that cost. Much of the service manager end of our company is comprised of the highest quality support staff and management pros, and we are certainly not the cheapest in that area. The two ways we are able to be more competitive is by cutting our profit, and we are very fair about that. The other way is to offer our artisans and trades more and regular work in exchange for a lower labor cost. Many times, our painter is also our tile setter. The paint job, stand alone, would be one price as would* *be the tile work. If I combine them, the artisan gives me a lower price in each category because his costs for doing the jobs are combined in many cases. I have done that here. If I itemize, I will have to price each aspect of the proposal as a stand-alone event. This means I can no longer offer you the lowest price I can. Do you see why it is impossible for me to itemize the costs and remain competitively priced?*

Buyer: *That makes sense, but I still want a lot of detail.*

Seller: *Absolutely you do. Your proposal will be very detailed respecting the scope of work and the finishes you will receive. Is that what you mean?*

Your product or service may not be as complex but notice how the objection was handled reasonably and sensibly. Your buyer will understand your explanation. If you have done your work in the Warmup Q&A you will have established enough credibility to be believed.

Features, Benefits, Real Value Statement

As you cover the details of your proposal, you will share many features of the offer. If you cannot define how the feature applies to the buyer and how the feature will be of value, the buyer may not appreciate the cost of the feature. If the buyer cannot see himself or herself benefiting from the feature, it carries no value. If only a few features appeal to the buyer, or the buyer perceives only a limited number of features that apply to him or her, your price may seem high.

- **Feature** - an aspect of your product or service.
- **Benefit** - how the feature affects the buyer.
- **Real Value Statement** - personal gain from the benefit.

The importance of the Feature, Benefit, Real Value Statement cannot be overstated.

Below are examples of how to present a Feature, Benefit, Real Value Statement:

> ***Seller:*** *As a part of this offer, you will receive a free month of service for every year you are a customer. That means you will get the equivalent of $50.00 per year as a bonus just for buying something you have to own anyway. It's like receiving free money you can use on other important things, like a tank of gas for your car. Not a bad deal, huh?*

- **Feature:** ***A month of free service***
- **Benefit:** ***Receive $50 per year bonus***
- **RVS:** ***You can buy something important with the free money. Not a bad deal, huh?***

Make the feature one of personal value to the buyer. Reminder: Always follow a statement in sales with a tie down question.

Following our remodeling role play:

> ***Seller****: We will cover all floors with plastic, erect dust curtains, and broom clean every day. We protect your living areas and make sure your home is clean every night when you are occupying it after work hours. This means it is less likely your children will stray into the work area, but if they do, they will not be in danger of hurting themselves. That is important isn't it?*

- **Feature:** ***Floor covering, Dust Curtains and Broom Cleaning***
- **Benefit:** ***You have a safe and clean home every night.***

- **RVS: *Your kids will be safe even if they stray into the work area.***

Again, never make a statement in sales without following it with a question. Make certain the buyer sees value in the feature.

Pricing and Terms

When you get to the bottom line, take a moment to summarize the offer. Ask the buyer if you have covered everything you discussed at the previous meeting. Ask the buyer if there is anything else that he or she wants included in the scope of work, product offering, service agreement, etc.

Here is a sample close:

Seller: *Your budget was $20,000.00 We are a little above that number at $25,000.00. Is that a price you can live with?*

Buyer: *Wow. That is a bit more than we discussed.*

Seller: *It is. Your new bathroom will be beautiful. How soon would you like to start the project so we can meet the Thanksgiving deadline?*

Price Drops

Sometimes it is necessary to reduce the price to earn a sale. As a professional seller, I don't subscribe to price drops, but I have used them in special situations.

The first rule of the Price Drop is **Justification**. If you drop the price without giving a believable and compelling reason why you can do it, your credibility will evaporate immediately and completely. Without justification, the buyer will think, *What is the real price?*

The second rule of the Price Drop is **Urgency**. The price drop must reflect a condition of the discount. If there is no deadline to the price drop, the buyer will perceive that the first price was inflated, and your credibility will evaporate immediately and completely.

The final rule of the Price Drop is **Commitment**. You must get a commitment from the buyer that if you are able to discount the price, he or she will buy today. This is part of the urgency but is often disregarded because of the direct nature of the condition.

Close the Sale

After you share the pricing with the buyer, close the sale. Ask for the business. As I discuss in **Closes**, I rarely get a yes or no when I earn a sale, so I don't often receive a hard objection. Typically, if I get an objection, it tends to be more conditional. Commonly, the objection has to do with delivery, timeline, arranging for payment, etc.

Let's say that you close then receive your first hard objection.

The price is higher than my anticipated budget.

You use the ***Formula for Handling Objections*** then again attempt to close the sale.

If you met their budget number, and you should have elevated their budget expectations in the warmup Q&A, close the sale.

Here is how you might handle the close:

> ***Seller:*** *We agreed that to earn your business today, we had to be able to start the project as soon as possible and complete the work by Thanksgiving. We also agreed that our budget was to be no more than $25,000.00. We decided that if I were able to meet your budget number and complete the project by Thanksgiving, we would do this together. Congratulations, the price came in at $28,650.00 and I have put it in writing that we will achieve substantial completion by the day before Thanksgiving. Would you prefer the demo crew begin this Monday or would mid-week be better?*

If you are not in the remodeling business and your pricing is static, this is how you might handle the close.

> ***Seller:*** *The total for the offer is $653.98. To what address would you like that delivered?*

Another example is:

> ***Seller:*** *That is $46.99 per month for your new pest control service. What day is best for you to schedule your initial treatment, Monday at 10am, or would Wednesday afternoon at 2 work better?*

Post Close

Once the buyer has signed the contract, approved the agreement, or okayed the work, whichever is your term, help him or her out of the buying ether.

Although the buyer has made a decision, it is certain that he or she will experience **Buyer's Remorse**. You want to invest a few moments to help the buyer through it. You don't want him or her to experience anguish or pain over the buying decision alone. Many times, Buyer's Remorse become regret. Regret can result in a call to your office with a cancellation.

> ***Seller:*** *I want to thank you for being a customer. I would also like to congratulate you on making a difficult decision. All our customers made the same decision you did, under similar circumstances. Each of them told us later how glad they were that they did. I want to ask you a question I always ask each of my customers. What finally convinced you that we were the right company for you?*

The buyer will, at this point, give you the reasons he or she chose you. As the buyer answers, he or she is also justifying why he or she bought from you. Agree with each of the reasons and assure the buyer that the reasoning is sound and wise.

Finally, chat briefly about how the product will be of benefit to the buyer, talk about some of the details of getting the product to him or her, or when the project will start.

REFERRALS

I am a proponent of asking for referrals while the buyer is happiest with you. No matter how well your company performs after the sale, there is always a possibility that something may go wrong or perhaps a glitch may occur, nothing serious, but not a perfect experience for the buyer.

This is how you handle it:

> ***Seller:*** *As you know, much of our business is earned through referrals. Do you know anyone who might benefit as you have from our product? (Don't pause) Maybe a relative? Jack, you play golf, I hear. How many of your golfing buddies might benefit from the product? Jill, you work at Huge Telecom. Do you have any colleagues who might see the value of this product as you have?*

TALKING WITH THE B2B DECISION MAKER

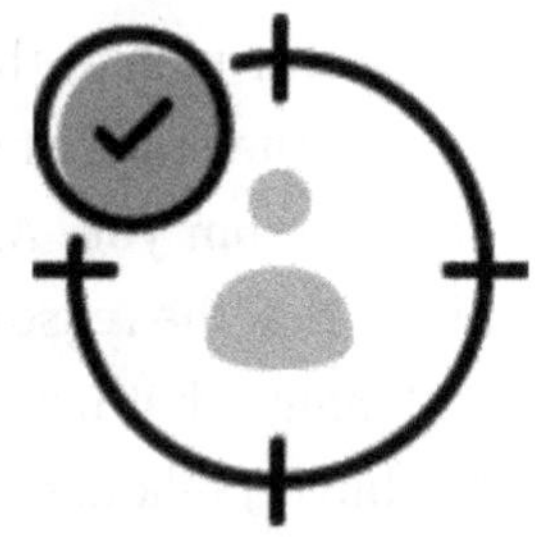

Every aspect of the B2B sales process is identical to any other sales process. If you are cold calling, prospecting is the only difference.

Do commercial consumers buy emotionally? As we discussed in **Chapter 1**, the buyer's decision to purchase a product or service is based upon many factors, among them is emotion. The sales process invests the buyer with confidence in the seller. This confidence comes from the seller's credibility and perceived motivations. The buyer will always pay extra for peace of mind. The buyer will always pay a bit more to someone he or she trusts and likes. The buyer wants to perceive value from the product. The buyer wants to be treated fairly and truthfully.

The more accurate question might be, do commercial buyers buy logically? Every purchasing manager or buyer agent has a list of his or her favorite vendors. Once in place, these purchasing professionals rarely bid out goods or services beyond that list. The purchaser has invested in those relationships and feels comfortable with those familiar vendors. Does that sound logical?

Buyers purchase from sellers. If the buyer likes the seller and perceives value in the relationship, he or she will pay more for the benefit of someone he or she trusts. Even purchasing directors/managers buy this way.

The Sales Process – Overview

The Sales Process seems complex. You probably have questions and doubts about its effectiveness. I understand how you feel. You have now seen behind the curtain. Being skeptical is a positive first step towards understanding and using the process.

The **Warmup Q&A** is the most important part of **Setting the Table for the Sales Process**. For the sales process to work, you must invest your time and effort in the preparation of the process. If you fail to earn **Credibility** through insightful **Qualifying Questions** and in the sharing of genuine interest in your buyer, the process will fail. The presentation and the **Features, Benefits, and Real Value Statements** will fall flat because you won't know where to scratch their itch. You don't want to scratch them all over hoping to find the itch because you didn't identify their areas of interest up front.

Once you become an expert on their needs, and they recognize that you invested the time in them to learn what they want or need, the buyer will necessarily invest you with the credibility you need to make the process work.

If you have not properly **Set the Table for the Sales Process**, when you handle their objections, pre-close, and attempt to close the sale, you will have no authority to do so. You will be perceived as pushy and high pressure.

If you have properly Set the Table for the Sales Process, you will succeed.

Pick and choose from the components of the Sales Process, like you are at an all you can eat buffet and you will fail.

IF YOU FAIL OFTEN ENOUGH AND YOU ARE DOING SOMETHING ELSE FOR A LIVING, YOU CAN ENTERTAIN YOUR FRIENDS WITH THE CLEVER TURNS OF PHRASE AND THE FUN SALES SLEIGHT OF HAND YOU LEARNED HERE.

If you learn the process and apply it to every sales call, you will earn a solid living while you gain the experience and instincts you need to become an elite seller, earning an executive income as you do.

In the **Introduction**, I shared with you that many books take the time to break down the psychology of sales for you. I don't believe psychology can be taught in a single book, nor do I believe a salesman is qualified to teach psychology. You will learn the mental aspects of the sales process over time. If you follow this process you will succeed.

The psychological components to which other sales trainers devote chapters, are built into this Sales Process. You will employ psychological tools without knowing you are doing it. However, if you don't use the entire sales process, many of the psychological tools will be missing or incorrectly applied.

[6]

CHAPTER 6 – ONE-CALL CLOSING

MANY OF US CONSIDER ONE CALL CLOSING an anachronism. No one buys on the first call, do they? Of course, they do. There are several industries, outside of retail, that base their sales process entirely on closing the sale on the first call. The most obvious are residential service industries.

Pest control companies feature door to door canvassing as a major part of their marketing/prospecting efforts. Others include roofing, lawn care, gutter cleaning, and often, handyman services. We will cover B2B one call closing later. For now, let's focus on the poor pest control salesperson.

I say poor because of the level of training of the typical salesperson rather than what he or she does for a living. Commonly, the seller is a college age youth with little to no sales experience.

Cold calling is the most difficult, and the most technical skill in the sales industry. Add **One-Call-Closing** to the load, and the seller is faced with an arduous climb indeed.

One of these pest control salesmen rang my doorbell a few weeks ago. He smiled as I opened the door. Immediately, he began his sales presentation.

It went something like this:

> ***Seller:*** *Hello, sir. I represent Acme Pest Control Services and we are doing some work for Frank here in your neighborhood and we thought we would make a special offer to you. We are performing the initial inspection and pest control treatment for half the usual price. After that, your service will cost $49.95 per month.*
>
> ***Buyer:*** *No thanks. I already have a pest control service, and they are doing a fine job.*
>
> ***Seller:*** *I noticed some wasp nests and spider webs in your eaves. Our initial service would eliminate them.*
>
> ***Buyer:*** *No thanks. I'm not interested.*

This conversation is the most common for these young sellers. The continual rejection discourages these upstart sellers, and few ever consider a career in sales because of the negative experience.

It may be because there is such a large turnover in the position that none of the sales managers who hire and train these youngsters teach them how to reduce the frequency of slammed doors.

As a professional seller and sales trainer, I took an interest in this salesman. I learned that his name was Josh. I asked him how sales were going for him. He confided that he wasn't doing well. He was in town for a couple of months until school commenced back east. I learned that he was trying to make money during the summer until he returned to continue pursuing his degree as an Engineer.

I was impressed with his career ambition and that he had chosen to try sales as opposed to waiting tables or delivering pizzas. I asked him if he was interested in a way to make his job easier and more successful. He looked at me for a long moment, with disbelief apparent in his expression before he agreed that he would.

I spoke with Josh for about half an hour. To his credit, he took notes and asked insightful questions. He became more comfortable with our conversation. I saw plainly that he was growing eager to try the new methods I was sharing with him.

At the end of our impromptu half hour sales seminar I said this:

"Josh, why are we getting along so well right now? It is because we have gotten to know one another, and we have learned that we are both interested in one another for mutual gain. You have picked up some valuable tips which may help make you better at your job. I have met someone with whom I genuinely enjoy talking. If you had met me with this same level of interest and friendliness, I might have bought from you."

"Do you think so?" he asked with surprise.

"Of course," I said.

Josh stood there for a moment. He was obviously uncomfortable.

"You should ask the question you are holding back", I urged him.

"What?" he asked with confusion.

"Close the sale," I urged. "My comment is a Buying Signal."

Josh obviously had no idea what I was talking about, but he asked, "Do you want to sign up?"

"If you sell four clients on my block, I'll be your fifth," I promised. "That is the price for your sales training."

He returned the following week and signed me up.

The Urgency – Key to the One Call Close

The Urgency in sales is poorly implemented more often than it is used effectively. The most common urgency is the **Disappearing Inventory Urgency**. The second is the **One-Time Price Urgency**.

Both can be effective, and both can immediately ruin the seller's credibility. As with the close, the urgency must be positioned in the initial contact portion of the presentation. An urgency works only when the product or service's value is established with the buyer, the buyer shows a desire to purchase at some time, and the seller has earned the credibility to be believed.

If the urgency is delivered without the proper preparation, the claim will come off as pushy, insincere, and manipulative.

- THE URGENCY MUST OFFER A REASONABLE EXPLANATION FOR THE BUYER TO DECIDE TODAY.
- THE URGENCY MUST JUSTIFY A PRICE DROP IF IT IS A PART OF THE DEAL.
- THE OFFER MUST BE LIMITED TO TODAY, WITH THE UNDERSTANDING THAT NORMAL TERMS ARE AVAILABLE IF THE BUYER DECIDES TO NOT TAKE ADVANTAGE OF THE SPECIAL OFFER.
- THE OFFER MUST BENEFIT THE BUYER SIGNIFICANTLY.
- THE SELLER MUST NEVER EXTEND THE OFFER FOR AN ADDITIONAL TIME PERIOD TO SUIT THE BUYER.

The home improvement business had an urgency which worked well. It may seem cheesy, but it appealed to the buyer's intellect and reason.

> ***Seller:*** *Mr. Buyer, as you may know, our business is seasonal. During times of lower sales numbers, my company sends out key management and administrative staff to our customers. These individuals are able to make exclusive deals with the customer in order to generate immediate work. We are willing to sacrifice profit dollars in exchange for immediate work that will keep our crews working rather than building shelves or sweeping floors in our warehouse. If I offer you a special price and payment that fits in your budget, can you give me a yes or no to that special offer today?*

I don't recommend you use this urgency with your buyer, but it demonstrates the components of the urgency. I must stress the last component of the urgency. Never extend the urgency terms to suit a buyer. The urgency depends upon a measure of pain to work. If the pain is removed, so is the urgency to buy today.

The One Call Close Process - Residential

The most difficult parts of the One Call Close are the beginning and the end: The Cold Call and the Close. Credibility is more difficult to earn when you have so little time to earn it. You must provide the buyer with an Urgency in order for them to buy from you today.

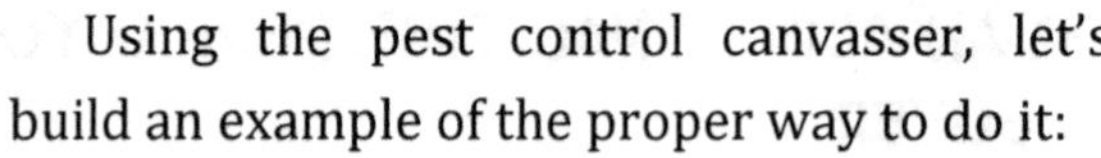

Using the pest control canvasser, let's build an example of the proper way to do it:

The homeowner answers the door where he encounters the pest control canvasser.

Seller: *Hello, sir. I am Josh with Acme Pest Control. What is your name?*

Buyer: *We are not interested.*

Seller: *Of course not, sir. I can only imagine how many times your doorbell rings and there is a salesman waiting there. May I ask you a question? How long have you been with your current pest control company?*

Buyer: *I don't know exactly. Maybe a few months.*

Seller: *It is common for homeowners to change pest control companies often. Most of my customers tell me that they change them frequently because of price. Has that been your experience?"*

Buyer: *I guess so.*

Seller: *It's interesting that most homeowners notice their pest control service only when they see bugs. That is the biggest reason they rarely think about the service. Most customers feel that if they don't notice bugs, that means their service is working. However, when my customers upgraded their pest control service to Acme, they found that we offer a higher level of service that is noticeable. We just started with one of your neighbors, Frank, from down the street. He found value in our service and signed up today. I am prepared to perform your initial inspection and treatment for half off our regular price if you upgrade your service today. Is this afternoon a convenient time to schedule your half-off initial inspection and treatment?*

Is the sale guaranteed? No, of course not. But what did the seller accomplish?

Josh kept the buyer at the door long enough to give his sales presentation. He asked qualifying questions and gave his presentation in a way that included the buyer in the benefit of his service. Josh built credibility and showed interest in the buyer.

Josh told the buyer how his customers benefited from "upgrading" their service to his company. Josh provided an urgency to buy today and attempted to close the sale.

Compare the presentation above to the pitch Josh gave me a few weeks ago. Which one is more likely to result in a sale? Which one is more likely to result in a higher number of sales? Which one is more comfortable for the buyer?

The One Call Close Process – B2B

One-call-closing businesses is more difficult than one-call-closing homeowners. The obvious reason is that when you knock on the door of a home, it is more likely that your first contact will be with at least one of the decision makers.

In business, you rarely meet with the decision maker initially. As we discussed in the **Cold Call** section, getting past the gatekeeper is the largest hurdle in the sales process. Once you meet with the decision maker, carefully crafted questions and a believable urgency will do most of the work.

To handle the gatekeeper, refer to **Chapter 2, Cold Call in Person - B2B**.

For our example, let's go with office supplies. Once you are in a meeting with the decision maker.

Here is how you handle it:

Seller: *Hello, Mr. Buyer. Thank you for taking a moment to meet with me.*

Buyer: *You're welcome, although I am happy with my current vendor.*

Seller: *Of course, you are. If you weren't, I would probably get a call from your office. The reason I dropped by today is because I have a question. Why do you buy your office supplies from an outside vendor rather than just going to the local office supply store?*

Buyer: *We don't have the time or personnel to chase something as small as office supplies. That is why we selected your competitor.*

Seller: *You hit it on the head, Mr. Buyer. Our customers go with us at first because of our competitive pricing. They stay with us, however, because we offer same day delivery and competitive price guarantees. Is that important to you?*

Buyer: *It is. You guarantee same day delivery?*

Seller: *Absolutely, on in-stock items, and our inventory is deep. When is your next office supply order coming due?*

Buyer: *We typically order at the end of the week.*

Seller: *That is only a couple of days away. I'll tell you what I'll do. If you place your weekly order with me today, I will include two reams of copier paper at no extra charge. Who oversees ordering your supplies?*

The decision maker will either accept your offer or give you an objection. Either way, you have the opportunity to earn his business today.

I AM HAPPY WITH MY CURRENT VENDOR

As cold calling professionals we are going to get our share of *disinterested* prospects. Remember that a put-off reaction by the buyer can be a sales process ender if you don't expect it and know how to handle it.

The *I am Happy with my Vendor* put-of is an objection. It is an early one, but an objection, nonetheless.

This objection is effective because it appeals to both the buyer's and the seller's sense of reason and fair play.

The buyer is portraying a fiction that he or she is loyal to his or her current vendor. The seller feels appreciation for any customer who would show loyalty to a vendor. Both of these are feel good reactions to a disingenuous objection meant to derail the seller's presentation.

This is an objection and is handled as such. The buyer probably feels no more loyalty to the current vendor that provides your product or service than he or she feels toward the convenience store where he or she last filled up with gas.

Here is how you handle the I am Happy with my Current Vendor objection:

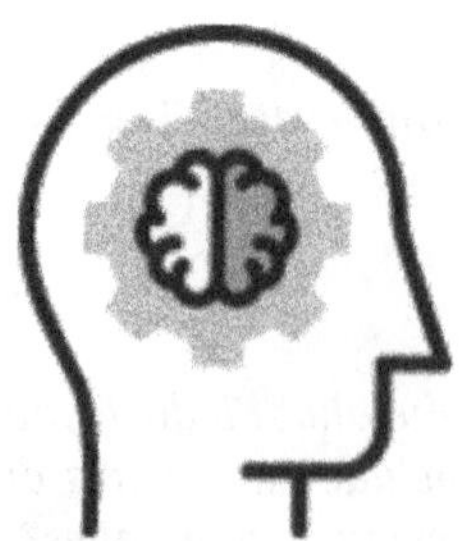

Seller: *Hello. Mr. Buyer, I am Craig with Acme Vendor. I would like the opportunity to compete for your business.*

Buyer: *I'm not interested, Craig. I am completely satisfied with my current vendor.*

Seller: *That is good to hear. I appreciate it when my customers are loyal to me. May I ask you a question before I go? How long have you been in business?*

Buyer: *We have been in business for 30 years.*

Seller: *I am familiar with your business, of course, although I didn't know you guys had been around so long. Do you have any clients you consider to be long term valuable clients?*

Buyer: *Of course.*

Seller: *When you started your business 30 years ago, isn't it true that many of those same clients you now consider valuable customers were not interested in you, your company, or your story?* ***(Don't pause)*** *But they did one thing. They extended to you the courtesy to listen to your story. Because they did, you now call them valuable customers. All I am asking, is that you extend to me the same courtesy and take a moment to hear my story. If at the end of 5 minutes you are still not interested, I will leave. Is that fair?*

This close appeals to the same sense of reason and fair play as the objection. The seller turns the tables on the buyer, presenting a personally relatable request. The buyer is placed in the seller's shoes by reminding him or her of the time a buyer presented the same objection to him or her.

[7]

Chapter 7 – Relationship / Hospitality Sales

SELLING GROUP-ORIENTED OR MEMBERSHIP TYPE clients requires a combination of retail sales techniques and direct sales tools. I call selling in this industry **Relationship Sales**. If you sell season tickets for sports teams, you are in the Relationship Sales business. If you work in Group Sales at a hotel or for an event services organizer, you are in the Relationship Sales business. Most commonly, hospitality sales, convention centers, meeting / wedding venues, or the rep selling gym memberships are in Relationship Sales.

I call this type of sales Relationship Sales because, unlike the salesperson selling a clearly featured product or service, the Relationship Salesperson must Set the Table for the Sales Process primarily by building rapport. The buying decision is rarely made in the seller's presence. As such, the seller must create a relationship with the buyer which makes the seller an invaluable part of the offer.

If the seller fails to set himself or herself up as an important aspect of the offer, the decision will be made upon price, bonus amenities, and the allure of the hospitality venue.

Salespeople in these industries would argue that price wins the deal. I disagree with that claim.

IF PRICE TRULY SOLD THE DEAL, THEN MOTEL 6 WOULD BE THE LEADING HOTEL CHAIN IN THE HOSPITALITY GROUP SALES BUSINESS.

If price truly were the main component in the decision, *Planet Fitness* would be the most popular workout center, and sports teams would never sell a single season ticket package.

I admit, in the hotel and event organizing business, my examples are overly simplified. It is presumed that the winning bid is the lowest price within a specific range of products or services determined by the quality levels of the amenities and the quality of accommodations.

Obviously, *Motel 6* would not bid against The *Ritz-Carlton* class of hotels for a group hospitality package. They are demographically too dissimilar. Amongst peer hotels, the sale is normally made based upon the lowest price, sweetened by special amenities, or value-added offers, designed to induce the buyer to purchase from them.

Hospitality Sales

I mentioned that Relationship or Hospitality Sales is a combination of retail and direct sales. Let's examine the premise.

In most cases, the group sales product or service is the same as the product or service offered individually. Hotel rooms, sports season tickets, and meeting spaces are all sold in individual units. Each is priced individually. The buyer can easily learn the price for the individual unit with a phone call, browsing a web site, or through many booking sites.

The buyer's impression is that group packages include a bulk discounted rate. The sector is sold that way by the sellers and purchased that way by the consumer.

As in retail, the buyer knows the price. The seller has little to offer as far as price motivation other than to discount the individual rate.

In retail, most big-ticket consumers enter a store with their online research completed. The Hospitality buyer knows what the price of a room or amenity is likely to be before he or she asks for a pricing package. Most hospitality sellers, like retailers, believe their only recourse is to offer bulk discounts and special offers of amenities and distinctive services.

Why do we accept the premise that price has nothing to do with our belief that *Motel 6* and *The Ritz* would never compete with one another, but we cannot agree that price has little to do with a competing sale made between like-hotels?

That's where the tools of the direct seller's **Sales Process** are effective. But rather than selling the buyer on the features and benefits of his or her product, the seller develops a rapport with the buyer. He or she builds a relationship with the buyer.

Even on the phone it is possible to gain the favor of a hospitality buyer. It is critical that the seller creates the first impression with the buyer as a valuable insider with the buyer's best interest at heart. Anyone who purchases for Corporate America will tell you that they have contacts in the industry who make their jobs easier.

The seller must present himself or herself as that helpful insider from the beginning. This is the one time that the seller displays his or her industry knowledge. Even if you are new at the Relationship Sales game, you can appear to be a knowledgeable industry insider. Knowing a lot about your product and service is important, but as we discussed in **Technical Expert vs. Sales Professional in Chapter 1**, don't let that knowledge get in the way of your sales process.

The **Warm-up Q&A** will create the perception for you. Your application of pain will confirm your knowledge of the dangers the buyer is attempting to avoid. Many veteran buyers for corporate America know little about how the Hospitality Industry works at the seller's level. Most consumers are just that. Sometimes a buyer for corporate has a background in Hospitality. When you encounter that person, include them in your circle of Hospitality Pros. Allow them to flex their knowledge muscle. People enjoy recognition of their skills and accomplishments. Including them as a peer is flattering and endears them to the seller.

As discussed in **Chapter 2**, Set the Table for the Sales Process. From the Warm-up Q&A through positioning yourself as an integral member of their decision-making team, the buyers must be treated in a considered way which creates that professional sales relationship few other sellers will bother to form.

It is common that a Relationship / Hospitality seller never gets the opportunity to present his or her proposal to the buyer. It is critical that the credibility piece is executed well so that when the sale decision occurs, the seller is a key factor in the decision.

Membership Sales

When you are enrolling new members at a gym, selling season passes for a sports team, offering season tickets for a theatre group, zoo, or civic organization, or offering member opportunities for a country club, the prospect will see inherent shortcomings to your offer.

The greatest is a **long-term contractual commitment** to a program or series of events. As sellers, we must understand that this reaction is not a genuine objection. It is fear of making a decision today on a product or service for which the buyer may not feel passionately about later. Anyone who has struggled over selecting a tattoo design knows the feeling.

WILL AN IMAGE OF A POPULAR BAND, PERMANENTLY INKED ACROSS MY CHEST, BE RELEVANT AND IMPORTANT WHEN I AM 65 YEARS OLD?

Most gym memberships are sold using a **Feature, Benefits, Real Value Statement** format. By a large margin, most gym membership sales are made from buyer walk-ins. The motivation to purchase a membership is already on the buyer's mind. The seller needs only to connect the features of the gym with the needs of the buyer.

In season ticket sales, if the buyer is an individual, the sale is dependent upon the buyer's enthusiasm for the team. Often, corporate buyers are interested in perks for employees and management, sales inducements for potential clients, or tax write-offs. For the business owner, a big motivation is Prestige.

How does the seller create a relationship with the buyer where the seller is important to the buying decision? As in hotel hospitality sales, the seller must present himself or herself as an insider, offering insider access to the buyer.

The individual buyer is a fan and wants greater access to the team. If the seller demonstrates that he or she is the agent by which that can happen, the relationship becomes important to the buyer.

The seller must earn Credibility and **Set the Table for the Sales Process** by using the **Warm-up Q&A**, and by delivering to the buyer a compelling presentation, tailored to address the needs and desires the buyer reveals through his or her answers.

Many season ticket sellers believe that the features and benefits of being season ticket holders are obvious. It is a given that the buyer is a fan. It is obvious that the buyer wants access to his or her sports heroes. These sellers rarely connect the season ticket offer to the buyer's dream. The sales presentation comes across as a list of amenities that come with owning season passes rather than a way to be a part of the team family.

What is the difference between a dream and a goal? *Zig Ziglar* said:

A GOAL IS A DREAM WITH A DEADLINE.

The buyer dreams of being a part of the sports team family. The buyer wants to see every game. The buyer does indeed want access. It is the seller's job to connect the dream with an attainable reality.

Two **Built-in Major Objections** with season tickets include: price and the number of games the buyer can attend. There are other objections, but those are the big 2. If the seller builds the value, and the buyer believes in the value, the sale will be made. The buyer will find a way to pay for the tickets and will certainly find a way to make the games.

Here are a few examples of questions the seller might ask the buyer:

Who is your favorite player on the team?

How many games do you attend each season?

How many games do you watch on TV?

How important is it to you to be a part of the team family?

How many games would you attend if you owned season tickets?

Who will be coming to the games?

These are sample questions, but they uncover a wealth of knowledge. The seller's questions in the Warm-up Q&A build an ownership impression in the buyer's mind. The buyer wants to *own* season tickets but the buyer fears *buying* season tickets.

The season ticket buyer and the gym membership buyer want to belong, but both buyers fear the purchase. If the ownership dream is stronger than the pain of the purchase, the buyer will buy the membership or season tickets. If your questions and your presentation create an ownership image in the buyer's mind, he or she is more likely to buy from you.

[8]

Chapter 8 – Question Forms

Questions Are the Answers in Selling

There is a saying: *What the seller says, the buyer tends to doubt.* Is this due to the bad reputation of the sales profession? Are people really that cynical about others? Is the Buyer Defense Mechanism stronger than the common belief that most people are good? I believe there is a bit of each in the doubting of a seller's honesty and integrity.

I believe that anyone, or organization, that needs to tout their integrity has an insecurity about them.

Mr. Gattis Pizza's slogan is *The Best Pizza in Town, Honest!*

Thou protest too much.

No matter the cause, the condition is genuine.

ANYTIME A SELLER MAKES A STATEMENT TO A BUYER IN A SALES PRESENTATION, IT MUST BE FOLLOWED BY A QUESTION.

If a seller makes the claim, *My company is the best company in town*, the buyer reacts instinctively, thinking of countless other companies that are better for a countless number of reasons. The buyer actively conjures from dim memories, or factual instances, any reason he or she can use to refute the seller's claim.

However, if the seller makes a statement, then invites the buyer to agree with the statement, only half if any of the typical disagreement energy is applied to refuting the claim.

As the seller sets the table for the sales process, any opportunity to get a yes, or even a degree of agreement from the buyer, helps to smooth the way towards developing the growing relationship between the two.

Here is an example:

What if I say to you, "Price is never the reason sales are lost?"

As a seller, you have just entered a mental phase of refuting the claim. Being a sales professional, you have a stake in the claim, and if you have been doing this for long, you are actively calling upon your memories of lost sales, and counting those you believe went to a competitor who offered a lower price.

Your natural sense of independent critical thought was activated at what you perceived as a challenge to your basic foundation, made up of your ideals and principles.

Here is the same claim, but this time it is followed by a question.

"Price is never the reason sales are lost. Don't you agree?"

Because I asked your opinion in the statement, your immediate reaction to search your foundation of ideals and principles is diminished because you are pleased to be included in the claim. It is a small difference, but if you defer to the buyer each time you make a statement, you will find that the buyer will ally with you more and more as the interview continues.

Asking for agreement is critical in sharing information that will ultimately lead to the buyer choosing you and your company. Although we all know that sales are lost to the lowest price every day, asking for the buyer's participation lessens the likelihood it will happen to you.

Questions Are Important in the Sales Process

Every question a seller asks, and the buyer answers, confirms that the buyer is going along with the sales process. Every question is a micro-close or a close in fact.

The type of question and the way the seller asks it determines the effectiveness and value of the question. Yes or No questions are the least effective because they require little effort for the buyer to reply.

Open ended questions require thought and consideration from the buyer. If the buyer is thinking about the seller's presentation and considering the offer from the standpoint of ownership, the odds are greater that the buyer will purchase from the seller. If an investment of thought and consideration is not asked for nor made, there is little chance for the sale.

A Note on Yes or No Questions

When a seller asks an open-ended question – one which cannot be answered with a yes or no – the buyer must necessarily think of a considered reply. The question serves to include the buyer in a conversation centered around him or her and his or her needs.

A YES OR NO CHALLENGES THE BUYER'S RESOLVE OR BELIEFS.

When the seller asks the buyer to say yes or no to a purchase, the buyer perceives the question as confrontational. The Buyer Defense Mechanism activates, and the buyer resists the sale.

If the seller has included the buyer in the conversation, and used the tools in this book, the most natural result of the process is for the buyer to purchase.

Tie Down Questions

This is a tag question. It most often is phrased as "Can You, Do You, Don't You, Aren't You, Won't You, Will You, Isn't It.

Example:

"This is the perfect color for your carpet, don't you agree?

Interrogative Questions

An Interrogative Question is an open-ended question which cannot be answered with a yes or a no. It is most often phrased using words like: Why, What, Where, When, and How.

Example:

"What is the biggest issue you are trying to solve with this product?"

Ownership Questions

An Ownership Question is any question to which the answer confirms the prospect is buying. Many salespeople make statements or ask general questions which reveal information without encouraging a thought of ownership from the buyer. Sellers should always ask ownership questions to encourage the buyer to see himself or herself owning the seller's product. In Real Estate sales, while showing a home, many agents say, *This is the kitchen; This is the second bedroom*; or *This is the backyard.*

Ownership is implied when a question is answered.

> *Example:*
>
> *Whose bedroom would this be? On which wall would you place your bed? Where would you place the kid's swing set in the backyard?*

Agreement Questions

Used sparingly, yes and no questions can be useful in a sales presentation. During the body of a wordy presentation the buyer may tend to wander mentally. Agreement questions are little way stations where the seller keeps the buyer engaged.

> *Example:*
>
> *The knick knack, paddywhack aspect of the technical gobbledygook of this product is confusing. Does that make sense to you?*

Closing Questions

A closing question is almost any question the seller asks during the sales process. A **Trial Close** question confirms that the prospect is buying the seller and the presentation. A **Hard Close** question confirms that the buyer is purchasing the product or service. Some are simple. Some are complex. Each should be clearly defined as one to which an answer is a commitment to purchase.

Examples:

May I have your order today?

In addition to the price, is there any other reason we are not going ahead with the sale?

If you could convince yourself that the price is fair, would you place your order today?

Challenging Questions

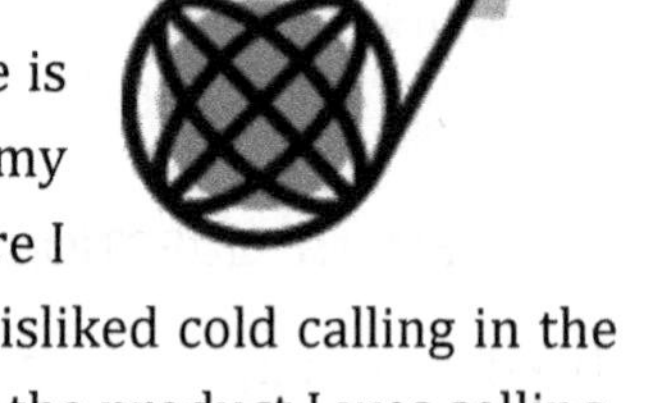

A Challenging Question is a question the seller receives from the buyer. Often, a Challenging Question is an objection phrased as a question.

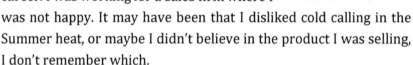

One of the best examples I can provide is a personal experience from early in my career. I was working for a sales firm where I was not happy. It may have been that I disliked cold calling in the Summer heat, or maybe I didn't believe in the product I was selling, I don't remember which.

I was Driving home after another unsuccessful sales day and I decided I needed a change. As I drove, I saw a *Nissan* dealership just off the freeway. I had worked as a car salesman early in my career and it occurred to me that I should give it another try.

I had my reservations about the long hours and a sales process where I had to be a management to buyer go-between, but I had been moderately successful before. With my experiences since, I felt certain I could make it work. I pulled into the dealership and walked into the showroom.

I was dressed in slacks and a golf shirt. Most of the men on the showroom floor wore ties, but undaunted, I pressed forward, committed to sell the sales manager on hiring me off a cold call interview. I believed myself a professional seller and I had no doubt that the sales manager would recognize my quality from the first moment we met.

I asked the receptionist to summon the sales manager and I waited, looking at the shiny new cars. I waited no more than five minutes before a stern-faced man in an expensive suit approached me.

"Can I help you", he asked.

"Hello", I said with a smile. "I am a professional salesman and I would like you to hire me to sell cars for you. I am experienced in car sales and I believe I could be a top salesman with your dealership."

"How can you claim to be a professional salesman when you are not even wearing a tie?" he asked cynically.

I am embarrassed to admit that I stammered as I struggled to explain that I was not wearing a tie because I was on my way home from work and my company didn't require me to wear ties, but...

I left with my tail between my legs and the following day, went back to work at the same job I hated.

The sales manager had asked a **Challenging Question** and I failed to use my sales tools to handle it. Some professional seller, huh?

This is how I should have handled the sales manager's challenging question:

Manager *Can I help you?*

Craig *Hello. I am a professional salesman, and I would like you to hire me to sell cars for you. I am experienced in car sales and I believe I could be a top salesman with your dealership.*

Manager: *How can you claim to be a professional salesman when you are not even wearing a tie?*

Craig: *Are you saying that if I wear a tie, you will hire me today?*

I employed a **Qualifying Question** in my response. Does it guarantee that the sales manager would have hired me? No. However, by qualifying his Challenging Question, I regained control of the interview and caused the sales manager to specify the terms under which he would hire me.

In this case, as a professional sales manager, he probably would have been impressed with how I handled a hard objection and would have hired me on the spot.

When a buyer asks a **Challenging Question**, it is an objection and a buying signal. **Qualify the question** and **Close the Sale**.

SAY "*NO*" QUESTIONS

The most common Say *No* Question is ***May I help you?*** Most retailers are wise to the automatic *No* this question elicits and have become creative. The clever retailer now asks the question using the interrogative, ***How may I help you today?***

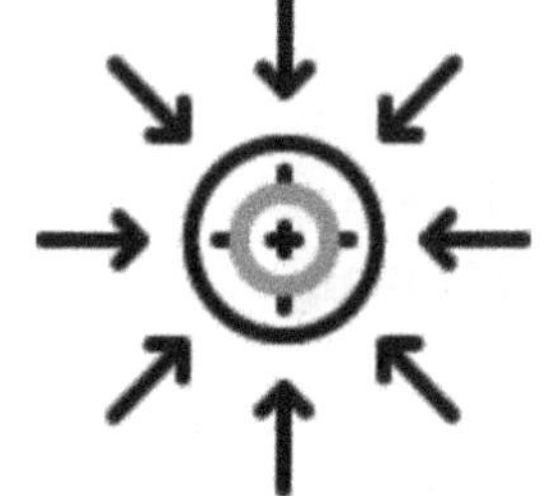

Both are **Say *No* Questions**. The first elicits a direct ***No***. The second gets a wordier ***No***.

The *May I help you* question occurs at the very beginning of the sales process. The *No* we want to avoid as sellers is the *No* to the beginning of the sales process.

If we don't **Set the Table for the Sales Process**, we will never gain the trust of the buyer. When we make first contact with the buyer, rather than asking if the buyer needs help, ask a different question which confirms the reason he or she is visiting the store.

This is a better way to greet a customer:

> ***Seller:*** *Hello, I'm Craig. Welcome to Acme Retail. Thank you for coming in to look around. What department can I direct you to?*
>
> ***Buyer:*** *We are looking for the electronics department.*
>
> ***Seller:*** *Of course. The electronics department is at the rear of the store. In the market for a new TV?*
>
> ***Seller:*** *Actually, we are looking for Home Automation.*
>
> ***Buyer:*** *Home Automation is a popular product today. Follow me, I'll take you right to the Home Automation aisle.*

Notice that the seller brings up the built-in-major-objection, *No thanks I'm just looking* when he says *Thank you for coming in to look around.* He then asks what department they are looking for which gives the impression that he has let the buyer go unhindered.

> *Thank you for coming in to look around. What department can I direct you to?*

Next the seller makes an **Error in Conclusion** statement. When the buyer corrects him, the seller is included in the sales process.

> *The electronics department is at the rear of the store. In the market for a new TV?*

Without asking if the customers need help, the seller is now helping them. The seller confirms the reason for the buyer's visit, compliments him or her, then begins the sales process.

Review – Question Forms

Questions should never appear to be an interrogation. Interviews, surveys, and interrogations are never pleasant experiences for a buyer.

Questions should occur within the smooth flow of conversation and represent genuine interest in the buyer's needs. Questions, most importantly, confirm to both buyer and seller that both parties are moving together through the Sales Process.

When a buyer answers a question, the seller must acknowledge the answer and tie it to a feature of the product or service. This will personalize the product for the customer more effectively than a presentation monologue.

[9]

Chapter 9 – Buying Signals

MANY SALESPEOPLE RECOGNIZE BUYING SIGNALS. Most fail to act upon them. Whenever you see or hear a buying signal from the buyer, close the sale. This may sound premature and a bit presumptuous, but trial closes train the buyer to open up to the seller.

The close may be a **Trial Close**, but the seller must acknowledge the **Buying Signal** during the sales process. Some Buying Signals are subtle, others are obvious. Most are unconscious reactions.

IF THE SELLER DOESN'T ACKNOWLEDGE THE BUYING SIGNAL WITH A CLOSING QUESTION, THE BUYER WILL NOT KNOW HE OR SHE IS SHOWING BUYING INTEREST.

By revealing the buyer's interest, the seller helps confirm the buyer's approval of the product or service as it struck him or her strongly enough to elicit a buying signal.

Remember, the buyer is in full **Buyer Defense Mechanism** mode. The emergence of agreement should be pointed out to help power down the Buyer Defense Mechanism.

Overt Buying Signals

Overt Buying Signals are those which can be seen or felt by the seller. A physical manifestation by the buyer, the seller must attempt to close each time he or she sees an overt buying signal.

Questions

The most common buying signal is a question. A buyer will not ask a question about a product or service if he or she has no interest in the subject of the question. Questions indicate interest.

Sample Close

> ***Buyer:*** *Can I get it in blue?*
>
> ***Most sellers will answer this question with a yes or no. Do not do that.***
>
> ***Seller:*** *Do you want it in blue?*

Objections

The second most common buying signal is an objection. A buyer will never object to something for which he or she has no interest. **See Chapter 8, Handling Objections.**

Subtle Buying Signals

Subtle Buying Signals are easily noticeable but are sometimes only variations in the conduct or manner of the buyer. The seller must attempt to close each time he or she sees a Subtle Buying Signal.

Emotional Reactions

Many times, a buyer will smile, frown, nod, or shake his or her head. These reactions are buying signals.

Sample Close

> ***Buyer smiles or nods his or her head.***
>
> ***Seller:*** *This color would look great in here, don't you agree?*

Gestures

The buyer may touch the product or handle a brochure.

Sample Close

> ***Buyer looks at a page in the brochure.***
>
> ***Seller:*** *Which of the three examples there catches your eye?*

Signs of Agreement

The buyer may smile, make an agreeable noise, or look to another decision maker.

Sample Close

> ***Buyer grunts at a statement the Seller makes.***
>
> ***Seller:*** *You are right. This is one of the more impressive features of this product. Where would you use it most?*

Physical contact

The buyer may pat the seller's shoulder or arm.

Sample Close

> ***Buyer pats the seller on the shoulder.***

Seller: *Wouldn't you agree that it is important to do business with people you like and trust?*

Summary – Buying Signals

Buying Signals are the reward for a solid **Sales Process**. These small cues indicate a growing comfort level between the buyer and the seller. Until the buyer takes ownership of a product or service in his or her mind, he or she will never own it in fact.

Other than the seller's **Credibility**, the most common reason a buyer displays a buying signal is because the seller has connected a feature/benefit of a product or service to the buyer's needs or desires. **See Chapter 2, Features, Benefits, Real Value Statement.**

[10]

CHAPTER 10 – CLOSES

CLOSES ARE NECESSARY AS BREATH, and dangerous as a lack of it. In the early days of modern sales, memorizing closes was a condition of employment for most sales organizations.

On a side note, it may seem funny to call any company a sales organization. Most companies sell products or services. Most people believe the product or service defines the business. Except for grocers, utility companies, and other need to own products, sales is an integral component to participating in a competitive marketplace.

Back when I was a *One-Call-Closing Tin Man*, we sold home improvement products, but make no mistake, we were a Sales Organization. Our products were merely a vehicle by which we plied our trade.

Our sales process was a Ten-Step Presentation practiced upon warm leads generated from a large "phone room." Telemarketing was king in those days before *Do-not-Call-Lists*.

Prospecting was also a part of it. We *Five-Starred* every lead. That is, we cold called the house on each side of the lead address and the three homes directly across the street. There were heavy bonuses paid for *ARC'd* leads. **(Add-on, Referral, Canvass)**. We one-call-closed everyone. Our motto was *Be Backs are Bullsh**.*

Read the chapter on **One Call Closing**. My friends who door knock in the pest control and roofing businesses will benefit from **Chapter 6**.

So why dedicate a chapter to Closes? Because, as you graduate to an elite level, you will learn how to position the close so you can use it.

In my days as a siding and storm window salesman, closes were memorized, and role played. During our free time, we salespeople used them as jokes for our entertainment. We trivialized them because, without properly **Setting the Table for the Sales Process**, they are guaranteed to fall flat.

Closing the sale is one of the most misunderstood tools in sales. Some of these I list below are more for your entertainment than for use. I know many closes and seldom use them. Remember, if you present an inch, you will have to close a mile. If you present a mile, you have to close only an inch.

In order to serve each close, I will follow each with a short **Close Summary**.

The Close

DO NOT OPERATE WITHOUT THE PROPER SAFETY EQUIPMENT

When around colleagues, most professional salespeople refer to themselves as Closers. Hard Closers, Clever Closers, One-Call Closers, Master Closers, High Pressure Closers, and Non-Closers. All of these Closers are only as effective as how well they present their product or service.

Closing the sale begins the moment you enter the buyer's presence. Everyone has heard the trite saying ***Always Be Closing***: That's right, ***The ABC's of Closing***.

I brought it up. Now I want you to forget it.

What is the true meaning of Closing?

THE MOST NATURAL CONCLUSION OF ANY SALES PROCESS IS A SALE

Closing the sale is the effective use of the Sales Process. In that sense you are always closing. In the zip-up boots and derby hat context, closing the sale is when you get the buyer to surrender and say yes.

What is the most common misuse of the close?

The presentation is going well. The seller and the buyer are moving along smoothly. The seller decides that it is time to close the sale. He or she looks at the buyer and asks a dynamic question like, "Shall we go ahead?"

The buyer's face stiffens into an expression of discomfort and alarm.

The customer buys you and what you are doing. If you change anything about those things, you risk alienating the buyer. If the buyer notices the place where your smoothly flowing presentation, which includes the buyer with well positioned questions, ends and an awkward close begins, he or she will balk.

Most salespeople enter a closing phase in their Sales Process. This phase is a change from what the buyer has accepted and is comfortable with thus far: **Buyer Defense Mechanism** activated.

I have sold, more often than not, without the buyer ever giving me a yes or no.

THE SALES PROCESS IS LIKE A FIRST DATE

Let me tell you a classic story. In today's sensitive social climate, I hope you forgive the old-school nature of my example.

A young man picks up a pretty young woman at her front door. They go to a nice restaurant, then to a movie. They leave the movie, chatting as the young man drives her home. He walks her to her front door.

The next moment is the best indicator of how the date went. **Here are the two possible outcomes:**

Outcome 1

The young man says goodnight to the pretty young girl. She smiles and says she had a good time. There is a pause as they spend an awkward moment struggling with how they should part company.

Finally, the girl says, "Well, goodnight. Thank you for a nice evening."

The boy searches his mind for something to say that will give him a chance to see her again. As she turns to the door he asks, "Can I see you again?"

The girl shrugs and replies, "I don't think so. Thank you anyway."

She opens the door and disappears inside the house.

Outcome 2

The couple stops at the door. Both say how much fun they had. After a short pause, they lean in and share a goodnight kiss.

The boy says, "We should do this again."

The girl says, "We should. Call me."

Which outcome indicates a successfully closed sale? In **Outcome 2** did either party ask if it was okay to share a goodnight kiss?

The sale was assumed. The kiss was a natural next step in their new relationship. The relationship was created from the moment they met at her door and continued to progress throughout the evening. She enjoyed his company and their date. She liked and trusted him.

Outcome 1 indicates that the date did not go well. The young man may not have done anything offensive or even wrong. The relationship was lost and asking abruptly to see her again did not help his case. Asking for the kiss that should have been assumed would have been aggressive and unwelcome.

Assume the Sale

If your **Sales Process** is properly executed, you have presented your product or service, connecting features and benefits to the needs of the buyer, and you have asked questions throughout, your closing question will be as innocuous as *What day would be best for us to start the work, Monday or Tuesday?*

The conclusion of your Sales Process must embody the total of your Sales Process. The buyer must demonstrate trust and confidence in you throughout. Asking for the sale should be as smooth as the flow of the Sales Process.

As I have said, the buyer buys you and what you are doing. You give him or her the product or service for free.

Trial Closes

Trial closes are questions the seller asks the buyer when he or she displays a Buying Signal. As the name indicates, Trial Closes gauge the buyer's level of commitment to the Sales Process.

As always, the effectiveness of the Trial Close is in direct relation to the Credibility of the seller. If the seller has properly Set the Table for the Sales Process, the buyer will respond to the Trial Close with none or perhaps a small effect from the Buyer Defense Mechanism.

Below are examples of Trial Closes.

Buyer: How long would I have to wait for delivery?

Seller: We are 3 weeks out currently. If I could expedite the process and get it here earlier, would that earn your business today?

Buyer: Can I get it in blue?

Seller: What shade of blue do you prefer?

Buyer: I'm not sure this TV will fit on our wall.

Seller: Is that the only concern keeping you from buying the TV today?

If the buyer responds in the affirmative or agrees that he or she would buy if..., the seller must attempt to close the sale.

If the buyer replies with dissent or in the negative, acknowledge the resistance and review a relative feature and benefit and continue with the sales presentation.

Buyer: This model is what we like but it is more expensive, and we aren't sure about the color.

Seller: I understand how you feel. The model we are discussing is limited in color, but it carries the same robust features as the more expensive models. Which one of the others do you feel more completely fills your needs?

Hard Closes

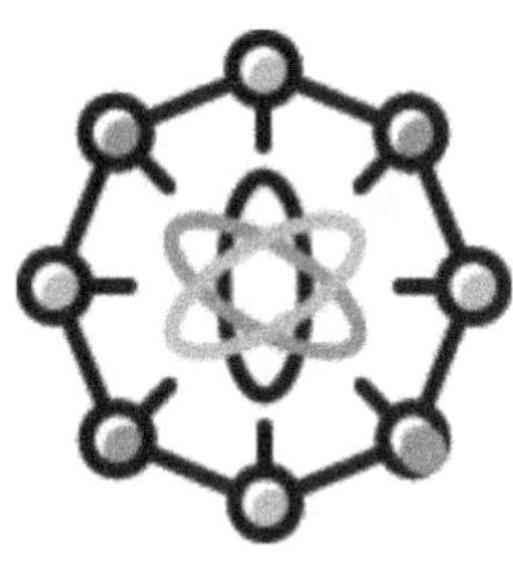

Calling these closes *Hard Closes* seems to fly in the face of our belief that high pressure is the stock and trade of the aggressive amateur. I call these closes Hard Closes for two reasons. The first is because the style of these Closes positions them necessarily at the end of the sales process. The second reason is to try the patience of those who consider any kind of close a Hard Close.

The most effective method of overcoming a fear of heights is to spend time at altitude. To alleviate a fear of closing, Hard Close.

As always, if the seller has not Set the Table for the Sales Process, and has not earned Credibility with the buyer, any closing question or tool will fall flat.

As promised, I have assembled a few Closes for you. I would remind you that if you present an inch, you will have to close a mile. If you present a mile, you have to close only an inch. If your Sales Process is sound, you will rarely have to use any close other than a simple question to sell. In the Close avoid asking a yes or no question of the buyer.

The first group of Closes are useful in many cases. The last couple of closes are for your entertainment only.

HIGH PRICE CLOSE – ALSO KNOWN AS REDUCE IT TO THE RIDICULOUS

Buyer: This lawn mower costs too much.

Seller: Of course, it does. How much too much is it?

Buyer: Your competitor offered the same type mower for $200.00 less.

Seller: So, another company is trying to sell a similar mower with like features for $200.00 less?

Buyer: The features are identical, and it is $ 200.00 less.

Seller: Mr. Buyer, how long did you own your previous mower?

Buyer: It lasted about 5 years.

Seller: You got a longer than normal work life from that one. Did you like your old mower?

Buyer: It was a good one, but it didn't have a self-propel feature.

Seller: Yikes. I see why you are looking for a replacement. Most mowers last 3 years if they are taken care of. Do you feel like you will maintain this mower responsibly?

Buyer: Of course. That's probably why the old one lasted so long.

Seller: I agree. How often do you mow?

Buyer: Once a week in the Summer and once every two weeks in the winter.

Seller: I see. If this mower lasts you three years, that makes the price difference only $67.00 a year or around $8.00 per month. If you mow every other week on average, the difference is only $4.00. May I share a thought with you?

Buyer: Sure.

Seller: When Acme Mowers was founded 30 years ago, ownership pledged that every time a customer visited our showroom or we visited a customer, that we would do everything we could for our customers. Since then, our mowers have been the highest rated and best supported after the sale. Why would any company do as little for a customer as they could get by with?

Buyer: I guess to save costs.

Seller: So they can sell it cheaper? Don't you want to do business with a company who is committed to your satisfaction, or are you willing to risk for $4.00 that a company is going to do as little as they can get by with?

Buyer: That is a good point.

Seller: Whose name will the warranty be under, yours or your wife's?

Close Summary: The components of the High Price Close are these:

- Confirm the price objection, clearly defining it.
- Agree with the buyer. If you disagree or tell the buyer a reason why he or she is inaccurate in his or her opinion, you risk a confrontation. A confrontation will result in the buyer feeling that you are arguing. Instead, simply agree with the buyer.
- Ask the buyer how long he or she plans to own the product. Never ask how long they plan to use it or, in the case of a home or car, how long they think it will last.
- Divide the difference in price into the time they give you. If you are selling tires, figure in miles. If it is a mattress, use nights, etc.
- Reduce the difference in price to the ridiculous.
- Tell your company story and how your product exceeds the quality of its competitors.
- Ask why the customer would risk, for the reduced difference in price, buying an inferior product or lesser company. No matter the answer, translate it as *So they can sell it cheaper?*
- Close the sale. The example above incorporated the *Order Blank Close*

THE CONTINGENCY CLOSE - ALSO KNOWN AS THE CALL THE OFFICE CLOSE

> *"Mr. Buyer, I'm not sure if I can get approval for this offer. I will have to give the office a call to go ahead with this. I am just warning you; I think they will say no. Before I call and put my job on the line, I want to ask you a question. If I can get this done, do we have a deal today?"*
>
> *When you get a commitment and the manager answers, say this, "Mr. Manager, I have Mr. Buyer here with me. Mr. Buyer loves the product, but he needs your help to move forward today. The Buyer says that if we can do A-B-C, he will buy today, isn't that right Mr. Buyer?"*

Close Summary: Typically, this Close follows a price drop. Remember, if you drop your price, you must justify the drop. If you lower the price without a reason why it benefits your company, the buyer will think, *What is the real price?* Your credibility will go out the window. Do not call the office until the buyer has given you a firm commitment. Often, it is wise to have all the paperwork completed, contingent on management's decision.

ORDER BLANK CLOSE

At the end or your sales presentation, begin filling out the contract or order form asking questions:

> *"What is the correct spelling of your name? Are we using your home address? Which cell phone number do you want for a contact number? Etc."*

As long as the buyer doesn't stop you, he or she is buying.

Close Summary: I genuinely like and believe in the **Order Blank Close**. Reading it like this, I am sure it sounds very salesy and pushy. In my career, I have sold millions of dollars' worth of goods and services without ever forcing the buyer to give me a yes or no. Remarkably, most sellers believe they must get a firm decision from the buyer before they can move forward with the contract. Remember the discussion we had on creating pain for the seller? Do you also remember the Buyer Defense Mechanism? This close falls under the category of Assume the Sale. It also embodies the trite saying we have all heard: *the ABC's of closing are Always be Closing.* Don't put the buyer's arm behind his back and make him say uncle. The buyer is generally on your side and is looking for an easy way to own your product or service. If you force a decision, you will engage his Buyer Defense Mechanism.

SECONDARY QUESTION CLOSE

> *As you hand the contract to the buyer to sign you say: "Can I get your signature today. By the way (control phrase), Would you like to use your pen or mine.*

Close Summary: This closing technique can be useful if you are causing pain as a part of building your rapport. It is more of a tie down than it is a final Close technique. If you are selling B2B, for instance, get traction with the gatekeeper by saying, *Gatekeeper, who makes the buying decision for this product or service? By the way, how long have you been with your current vendor?*

If it is said thoughtfully and sincerely, your sales presentation may seem less canned.

ALTERNATE CHOICE CLOSE

> *"I am available this week? Which is better for you, 10am on Monday or would you prefer something later in the week, say Thursday at 2?"*

Close Summary: In the presentation, this close will help the customer reveal buying interests and choices that will indicate what they are wanting to buy from you. *Mr. Buyer, if you were to purchase today, which would you select, option A or option B?* Compliment their choice.

Error in Conclusion Close

When the customer tells you, they want to do things a certain way, this close helps to confirm they are genuinely interested or reveal that they are merely trying to postpone the buying decision.

> *"Mr. Buyer, what you are saying is that if I can deliver by Monday, you will buy two cases today?" Customer: "I said I would buy one case today." Seller. "Great. Let's get that delivery scheduled. What is the shipping address?"*

Close Summary: This is a great tool if you assume the sale - and you should always assume the sale. The buyer is at the decision stage and you ask them what it would take to earn their business today. They give you a non-committal response. Clarify the terms of their potential buying decision. When they agree to the hypothetical, make an error in their perceived terms. Once they correct you, close the sale.

Novelty Closes

The following closes are real but were used only by a bygone era of slicksters.

Ben Franklin Close – also known as the Balance Sheet Close

If a customer is having a difficult time making a buying decision, offer to assist them.

> *"Mr. Buyer, you have heard of Ben Franklin, one of our country's founding fathers? He published a periodical called Poor Richard's Almanac. In one of the issues he offered a technique for making difficult decisions by employing reason and logic to the issue. He drew a T on a piece of paper. Above the 'T', on the left Side of the vertical line he wrote 'Yes.' On the right he wrote 'No.' Below each he would list each reason why he should make a yes or no decision. Why don't we try that? "*

The seller draws the *T* and writes *Yes* above the left side and *No* above the right. Now begin listing all the Yesses. The seller will help by offering suggestions for the yes column.

Once that column is filled, pass the page to the buyer, and ask him to list the Nos. The seller must not offer any *No* ideas. When there are far more reasons in the *Yes* column, close this way.

> *"Well, Mr. Buyer. It seems that the decision is clear. What is the correct spelling of your name?"*

Close Summary: There is no reason whatsoever to use this close. If your buyer is having this much trouble making a decision, ask them what is troubling them. Review the particulars of your offer.

The Colombo Close – also known as the Dying Swan Close

If you have a customer who just won't gel (buy), thank them for their time and express your regret that you were not able to help them. Pack your sales kit and head for the door. When you reach the door, place one hand on the knob as if you are about to leave. Pause and turn to the Buyer touching a hand to your forehead, like *Colombo* used to do before he solved the caper, and say the following:

> *"I'm sorry Mr. Buyer, but as you know I make my living as a salesman. Could you help me please? What is it about the offer did I not cover well enough for you to see that this is a great deal? What did I do wrong? I could really use your advice."*

Once the buyer discloses the error or the reason they didn't buy, say *Oh, I didn't cover that? No wonder you still have questions.* Return to the meeting area and close the sale.

PETER FAULK IS THE ONLY GUY WHO EVER MADE THIS SCHTICK WORK. DON'T TRY IT.

[11]

CHAPTER 11 – HANDLING OBJECTIONS

MOST SELLERS DREAD AN OBJECTION. To the amateur, objection equals rejection. We pro's see an objection as an opportunity. An objection is an opportunity to close. An objection identifies a point of interest.

A buyer will never object to the color if color is unimportant to him or her. A buyer will never object to a delivery date if he or she is not rushed to receive the purchase. A buyer will always object to something he or she cares about or is interested in. As with Buying Signals, Objections indicate a point of interest. There is one exception to this rule, the *I Need to Think About It ob*jection. Read about that one at the end of this chapter.

If the buyer doesn't object to the price, there is no interest to buy. When the buyer objects to a feature or benefit of the product or service, the buyer is interested in how the feature will impact him or her if he or she buys.

As with Buying Signals, when you receive an objection, use the **Formula for Handling Objections,** and close the sale.

Two Types of Objections – Major and Roadblock

An objection is a Buying Sign. When you receive an objection, you must determine if it is a Major Objection or a Roadblock Objection. A Major Objection is a buyer's concern which, if unanswered will kill the sale. A Roadblock Objection is a buyer's effort to slow down the process. The Roadblock Objection is generally a product of the Buyer Defense Mechanism.

Major Objection

A major objection is a genuine concern the buyer has about your product or service. This concern means he is taking your presentation seriously and sees value in it. It is likely your presentation elicited the objection through a lack of information or a lack of clarity on the issue. Sometimes the objection comes from a buyer's preconceived idea about your product of service.

Door to door pest control sellers run into this all the time. The seller rings the doorbell. A stern-faced homeowner opens the door. The seller begins his sales pitch. The stern-faced homeowner informs the seller that they already have a pest control service and *We are not interested!*

The seller knows that, as in all service-based products, pest control services are not equal. The objection is based upon a preconceived notion that they are. By the way, this is also a **Built-in Major Objection**.

Built-in-Major-Objection

The largest Built-In-Major-Objection for any product or service is the seller. The buyer doesn't often name the seller as an objection as they would price or color, but they react negatively to any salesperson who approaches them, invited or not.

There is a belief that people automatically input a negative into an unknown. If you are in a meeting with a client, and the buyer takes a call then immediately excuses himself or herself from the meeting, what is your first impression? You would probably assume something is wrong and the buyer was called away to attend to the matter. How likely is it that your first guess would be that the buyer had just found out he or she had just inherited millions of dollars and had to leave to claim it? No one would.

The buyer is no different and will input a negative into an unknown when you are selling.

I was the sales manager and marketing director for a telecom company. We advertised that if our customers experienced a service failure, we would repair the failure for free and prorate their service for the entire day.

The feature was a hit, and our competitor lost customers in droves as they switched to our service. Ironically, we copied the free repair feature directly from the competitor. Because the competitor didn't talk about it or sell it to their customers as a feature, the buyer assumed the service feature was not available. The buyer inserted a negative into an unknown.

In the case of a Built-in-Major-Objection, the seller must bring it up first and make it a feature of the product or service.

If you are selling green electric cars with pink polka dots, the last thing you want is for the buyer to say, "Good god, that is a green electric car with pink polka dots." You want to present the color as a feature. "We build only green electric cars with pink polka dots, and this is why it is important to you."

If you hide the objection from the buyer, or worse, ignore the issue, the buyer will turn the unspoken issue into a negative conclusion to the sales offer.

Roadblock Objection

Invariably, the Roadblock Objection is the buyer's attempt to slow down the sales presentation because he or she is close to a buying decision. This objection is typically valid but is not a deal killer.

An example of a roadblock objection is the retail version. *No thanks, I am just looking.* Although it is a Roadblock Objection, this one is the most common and perplexes most sellers. When a buyer says, *No thanks, I am just looking,* does it block the sale? Of course not. The buyer is rejecting an unwelcome advance by a stranger who also happens to be a seller. The buyer entered the store with purchasing a product on his mind.

The Formula for Handling Objections

Differentiate between Major Objections and Roadblock Objections.

1. **Ignore the objection**
2. **Acknowledge the objection, then return to your presentation.**
3. **Reflect the objection but worded as a question.**
4. **Isolate the objection.**
5. **Answer the objection**
6. **Confirm the answer.**
7. **Close**

The following example is an abbreviated presentation. Remember, the objection may not come up again for several minutes as the presentation progresses.

Here is an example:

Buyer: *I'm not sure about your company's cell coverage in my area.*

Seller: *Yes, sir. Your service will include a new phone at no cost just for signing up.*

Summary: If, during the seller's presentation, the objection doesn't come up again, it is a roadblock. If it returns, it may be a concern but not a deal killer.

Buyer: *I am concerned about the coverage in my area.*

Seller: *I understand how you feel, sir. We have the most complete coverage in the industry.*

Summary: The second time, the seller acknowledges that he heard the objection using the Control Phrase *I Understand how You Feel.* If given the chance, the completed presentation might clear up the objection. The seller must continue building the sales momentum. The buyer will derail the seller's momentum if the presentation is halted to handle the objection.

Buyer: *I'm not interested if I can't get coverage in my area.*

Seller: *So, your biggest concern is that we may not have sufficient coverage in your area?*

Summary: The buyer presents a Buying Signal. A genuine concern is a genuine indicator of interest. Qualify the Objection by converting it to a question.

> ***Buyer:*** *That is correct.*
>
> ***Seller:*** *In addition to the coverage, is there anything else keeping you from signing up?*

Summary: Isolate the objection as the only thing standing in the way of the sale. If it is not the only objection, ask if there is any other reason not to proceed. After each objection ask, *Is there any other reason in addition to the (repeat the last objection) that you are not going ahead?*

> *Buyer: Nope.*
>
> *Seller: If you look at this coverage map, you can see that your home is in the center of our coverage area. Many other carriers don't have the coverage we do in rural areas. Does that answer your question?*
>
> *Buyer: Yes, it does.*
>
> *Seller: Excellent. Do you want to keep your current phone number, or would you like a new one?*

Summary: Answer the question, then tie it down with a Closing Question.

I Need to Think About It

The *I Need to Think About It* objection is the death knell of any sales process. There is a formula for handling it, but your chances of recovery are the same as Stage 4 cancer. It is possible that you can still get the sale, but the odds are worse than winning the lottery.

When a seller receives this objection, he or she has not done his or her job. This objection means that one or more components of the Sales Process are missing.

- DID THE SELLER EARN CREDIBILITY?
- DID THE SELLER CONNECT WITH THE BUYER DURING THE WARM-UP Q AND A AND ESTABLISH AN IMMEDIATE NEED?
- WAS THE SALES PRESENTATION DELIVERED WITH ADEQUATE AND IMPORTANT QUESTIONS, AND CONFIRMATIONS THAT THE FEATURES AND BENEFITS WERE IMPORTANT TO THE SELLER?
- DID THE SELLER ELIMINATE THE COMPETITION?
- DID THE SELLER GET A FIRM COMMITMENT AT THE FIRST APPOINTMENT FOR A YES OR NO TO THE PROPOSAL?

The loss of a sale to the *I need to Think About It* objection is the most frustrating of all. Maybe it is the lack of closure. Perhaps it is the blatant indictment against the seller and the skill the seller possesses.

If you find yourself faced with this hopeless objection, here is the response:

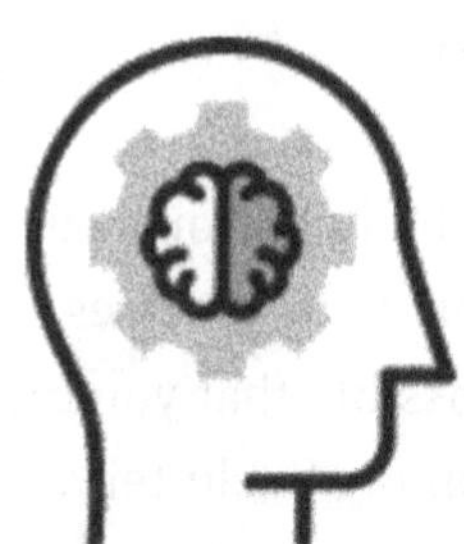

Buyer: *I need to think about it. We don't make snap decisions.*

Seller: *I completely understand how you feel. I am the same way. Just to clarify my thinking, may I ask you a question?*

Buyer: *Sure.*

Seller: *What is it particularly about the offer that you need to think over? Is it the color? Is it the size? Is it my company? Is it me?*

Don't pause between *What is it particularly about the offer that you need to think over?* and your itemization of each component of your presentation.

The last question is always, *Is it the price?* If you pause between the first question and your itemized list, the buyer will automatically respond, *The whole thing.*

If you are successful, and the buyer identifies the one thing he needs to think about, use the **Formula for Handling Objections** to isolate and close on the objection.

Control Phrases

You will become familiar with the term C*ontrol Phrases*. These are verbal switches that keep the buyer on track. If the buyer diverts the presentation towards an off-topic condition, the seller loses control of the presentation, and the momentum is lost. This is like an objection because, generally the diversion is the buyer's attempt to slow down the sales presentation, or is related to the buyer objecting to purchasing your product or service based upon the subject of the diversion.

If a buyer interrupts a sales presentation with a story about Aunt Julie's thyroid operation, the seller will need to get the conversation back on track to build or maintain the **Sales Momentum.**

A good Control Phrase is delivered this way:

"By the way, did I mention that we offer zero interest financing?"

By the way is the Control Phrase. When used, the buyer will pause, waiting for the seller to finish.

Allowing the buyer to take the conversation away from the presentation cripples the flow of information, and places importance on the new subject. Losing control of the presentation will result in a lost sale, or worse, the *I Need to Think about it Objection.*

The seller's credibility is undermined when leadership in the process is lost. Gently guide the direction of the interview with relevant and considered questions.

EXAMPLES OF CONTROL PHRASES:

By the way...

May I ask you a question?

You reminded me of something, and I think it may help...

That reminds me of something I forgot to tell you...

Joe (use the buyer's name) ...

I understand how you feel.

A Thought on Objections

The sales process is dependent upon an open, two-way conversation. As in any relationship, the power dynamic will naturally pass from one party to the other then back again.

Professional sellers understand the nuances for the control of this dynamic. If abused by either party, the struggle becomes a power grab. The ultimate power grab for the seller is represented by high pressure and pushiness. The ultimate power grab for the buyer is presented as hard objections and relegating the seller to the role of proposer and bidder. Neither is productive or positive.

A relationship requires a genuine warm regard and consideration for one another. The sales relationship you build with your buyer is no different.

The buyer will not perceive you as a participant in the relationship until you Set the Table for the Sales Process. The level of difficulty of the objection you receive, indicates the effectiveness of your presentation. The worst objection any seller can receive is *I need to think about it.* If you get this objection, as I said earlier, you did a poor job at the start.

IF THE SELLER IS ILL-EQUIPPED TO HANDLE THE BUYER'S STRUGGLE FOR CONTROL, HE OR SHE WILL SUCCUMB TO THE REVERSE POWER DYNAMIC, AND HE OR SHE WILL LOSE THE SALE.

It is the seller's responsibility to maintain the greater level of control. Sellers accomplish this by effectively Setting the Table for the Sales Process. The preparation must be completed before the sale is closed.

Keep in mind that the buyer wins when the seller prevails. If the buyer does not purchase from you, the alternative for the buyer is an extended ordeal of requesting prices and alternately rejecting or accepting the winning bid. Both ways result in the buyer purchasing a product or service. Why shouldn't the selected product or service be yours?

[12]

Chapter 12 – The Close (of the Book)

A SALES PHILOSOPHY IS A CONTROVERSIAL THING. Everyone seems to have an opinion. As with buyers today, businesspeople and sellers are better informed than at any other time in modern history. Creating a business in America has never been easier. A web site, a vehicle wrap, and a couple hundred dollars paid to an online legal service can result in an entrepreneur founding a corporation with a virtual storefront.

Sales is similarly practiced. If someone has been doing something for a long time, he or she generally claims expert status in the endeavor. What is the saying? *Practice doesn't make perfect. Perfect practice makes perfect.*

If the standard for being a skilled walker was limited to the moment a baby stands and crosses the room for the first time, no one would have ever run a 4-minute mile.

SELLING TO A BUYER DOES NOT INDICATE A SKILL IN THE CRAFT. OF THREE PROPOSALS, ONE WILL BE AWARDED THE JOB. THAT SALE DOES NOT INDICATE SALES ABILITY.

The seller who practices an effective Sales Process at its most advanced level will not sell every buyer he or she encounters. No one has a 100% closing record. Everyone misses sales. Everyone loses sales opportunities. The reasons are as varied as they are numerous. An effective Sales Process, performed adeptly, will improve a seller's closing percentage.

SUCCESS IS RARELY DETERMINED BASED UPON PERFECTION. THE TOP PRO BASEBALL PLAYER ACHIEVES AROUND A .300 BATTING AVERAGE. THAT MEANS HE FAILS TO GET ON BASE 2 OUT OF EVERY 3 TIMES AT BAT.

In the *NBA*, the average shooting percentage isn't much higher. *Michael Jordan*, one of the greatest players to ever play the game, achieved a .497 career field goal percentage. That means he missed more than half of every shot he attempted.

Professional athletes work at their craft tirelessly. More of their time is invested in preparing for a game than is spent playing in a game. In sales we must work tirelessly to perfect our craft. What is our craft? Our Sales Process is our craft. It is a means by which we maximize our efforts at every opportunity.

When I miss a sale, I take great comfort in the knowledge that my sales numbers are an inherent aspect of my profession. The commonly accepted closing percentage nationwide is around 33%. If you can improve your closing percentage, you will realize a significant increase in your income. When you miss a sale, recognize that the failure is a common and acceptable loss.

As in professional sports, ours is a profession of averages. Why do you think we are so handsomely rewarded? The job is difficult. The odds are long. The measure of success is based upon fractions, not wide margins.

When I entered the sales biz in the mid-eighties, I answered an ad in a newspaper offering a sales job claiming the applicant could make $10,000.00 a month merely by working 2 hours a day.

I was young and gullible, so I jumped on that one. At the time, I was a carpenter on a blisteringly hot construction site. I was making nowhere near that kind of money a month. I was making little more than that a year. The idea of working so little to earn so much was a dream come true.

It turned out that the 2 hours of work occurred only after many more hours of prospecting, cold calling, rejections, presentations, and proposal preparation.

I didn't accept that job offer, but the experience whet my appetite for sales. I was seduced by the word games and the wildly imagined possibility of success. That Summer launched me upon a journey that continues to this day.

In those days, a sales career was attractive to young people. That was a time before the devolution of social awareness - *Woke* - removed our young people's ability to think critically.

I fear sounding like my dad, but we weren't addicted to electronic devices and time-consuming apps. Work was our app. Our careers consumed our time.

Because of the popularity of sales, there was a need for real, hard-nosed sales training. I studied sales techniques night and day. I attended sales seminars by *Tom Hopkins, Zig Ziglar, Phil Storres,* and many other lesser known trainers. If my car was speeding down the road, it was certain that there was a cassette tape rolling, and sales training was blaring from the car stereo speakers.

I believed that if someone could do something, I could do it too. Since then, I have committed my professional sales life to achieving perfection in the Sales Process.

As with everything in life, perfection is unattainable. I believe that success is not the achievement of a worthwhile goal. Success is the continuing effort and journey towards achieving a worthwhile goal.

Once a goal is accomplished, another takes its place, and the journey begins once more.

Sales is rarely practiced at a professional level anymore. Social morality has taught us that personal interest is selfish; profit is a sin; and achievement is taking advantage in a zero-sum game.

Capitalism is not a zero-sum game. If you earn, it does not mean that someone else loses the same sum. There is room at the table for everyone and for anyone who chooses to practice the skills necessary to do so.

I hope that selling will become popular once more. I work daily to make sales the honorable and necessary profession it was meant to be.

MORE THAN FROM ANY OTHER CAUSE, PSYCHOLOGISTS TREAT PATIENTS WHO SUFFER FROM MALADIES THAT STEM DIRECTLY FROM DOUBT AND UNCERTAINTY.

As professional salespeople, we are in the business of helping others by helping to alleviate the pain of doubt and uncertainty. The anguish of indecision is a curable pain.

Salespeople have contributed much to the bad rep they receive. Any professional pursuit can be tainted by a lack of integrity. Why do doctors, attorneys, CPA's, first responders, and even soldiers take an oath, and adhere to closely monitored ethical and professional standards?

Anyone who is trusted by someone, is uniquely positioned to harm that person. Sales is one of a very few professions where the seller is in the position to manage the use of another's money and property while receiving personal gain but is not officially regulated or overseen in the pursuit of that profession.

The inherent danger the salesperson represents to the buyer is real and obvious. Those who have taken harmful advantage of that trusted relationship have muddied the water for all of us.

As a professional seller, it is your sacred duty to take care of the buyer. The buying decision is the most hazardous step the buyer can make. You must be truthful and honorable when that trust is placed with you. A large part of the attractive income sellers earn is paid for the seller's trustworthiness and principles regarding the sale.

I hope that the techniques in this book will contribute to your skill in helping the buyer through the difficulties of the buying decision. The greatest value of these tools is the trust with which the buyer rewards the seller, and the benefit the buyer receives for investing that trust wisely.

During my career, many of my colleagues, and often, my competitors, ask me how I am able to sell my product or service for so much more than everyone else. My answer is normally an abbreviated, but acceptable one, touting my presentation and closing techniques.

The detailed version is more accurate.

A sales offer has a finite number of components. Those include a product or service, the cost of bringing that product or service to market, marketing and sales costs, taxes, fees, and profit. All of these are customary and acceptable cost factors. All of them can be justified on a balance sheet. This is the point where most sellers stop.

The professional seller adds an aspect to the offering that most others know little about. Many in sales see this rare cost as selfish and greedy because their business view has no understanding of how and why a customer buys.

As professionals we recognize the value of our service to the buyer. We, like the buyer who is offered the service with a genuine regard and concern, see the great value in the cost.

Some generalize this component as *peace of mind*. That is an oversimplification. The truth is, when a professional seller develops a sales relationship with a buyer, the seller shares the burden of doubt and uncertainty with the buyer. A sales close is the logical and mutually desired conclusion to the shared journey. If the seller never enters the relationship and never shares the burden, the seller remains a part of the burden.

The psychology of sales is something I have heard about all my professional life. I don't understand the mechanics of it, but I do know how the mysteries of the human mind can impact a sale, positively or negatively.

I approach sales as I would any job. If you have ever attended a self-help seminar, you have participated in the games and drills designed to help you gain confidence or personal power. The tricks and deceptions we learn to perpetrate upon our minds, as we attempt to lessen the pain of rejection, solve nothing.

Does the carpenter have to look in the mirror and say *Cancel! Cancel! Sweep away!* before he or she leaves for the job site? The carpenter's obstacles and discomfort do not stem from a buyer slamming a door in his or her face. The carpenter's difficulties arise from working in hazardous conditions; suffering in the heat or cold; and daily bone-wearing fatigue.

In sales, our difficulties include rejection and memorizing, then executing, a detailed sales process, dependent upon perfect delivery.

Approach sales as a job that must be done to achieve significant gain. Hinge your perceptions of the job on the numbers. Know that while using an effective Sales Process, you will call on a certain number of prospects, and a predictable number of those will listen to your presentation. Of those who see your product or service, a forecastable number will buy. If you are following a reasonable and successful Sales Process, you can count on your sales numbers day in and day out.

Invest time today in learning the Sales Process. Tomorrow the Sales Process will allay the difficulties and fears of selling. With experience, your confidence in your process and your product or service will occur naturally and will be apparent to the buyer.

This book was the first step for you. Make the most of the tools about which you have read. If you do, you will earn a significant living while you gain the experience and the confidence that will make you an elite sales professional.

Good luck in your sales career.

ABOUT THE AUTHOR

Craig Rainey was born in San Angelo, Texas and now lives in Austin. A life-long sales professional, he has owned sales-oriented businesses, managed sales teams, launched sales departments, and has won numerous awards for his successes in sales. As a public speaker on sales and sales training, he prides himself on being one of the few public sales personalities who works every day in the sales business, not just at selling his training literature and training services. Craig is the author of three fiction novels as of this writing. He is an award-winning actor and screenwriter.